PENGUIN HANDBOOKS

# BEGINNING CHESS

Harry Golombek was born in London in 1911, and educated at Wilson's Grammar School and London University. He became boy chess champion of London in 1929, and two years later was the youngest player ever to win the Surrey Championship. He is one of Britain's leading players, and figured fourteen times in the prize list of the British Championship, from equal second in 1938 to first in 1955. He was British Champion in 1947, 1949, and 1955. He is also one of Britain's foremost international masters, and was captain and first board of the British team at the Helsinki International Team Tournament 1952, captain at Amsterdam in 1954, first board in Moscow in 1956, and captain again at Munich 1958, Leipzig 1960, and Golden Sands 1962. He has written books on many aspects of the game, and is recognized as Britain's leading theorist. An authority on rules, he was appointed by the International Chess Federation to act as judge at the World Championship matches in Moscow 1954, 1957, 1958, 1960, 1961 and 1963. He has translated *The Art of the Middle Game* by Keres and Kotov, which is published in Penguins. He is Chess Correspondent of *The Times* and he was awarded the O B E in 1966 for services to chess. Harry Golombek is also known as one of the team that broke the Enigma code in the Second World War.

HARRY GOLOMBEK

# BEGINNING CHESS

PENGUIN BOOKS

Penguin Books Ltd, Harmondsworth, Middlesex, England
Penguin Books, 625 Madison Avenue, New York, New York 10022, U.S.A.
Penguin Books Australia Ltd, Ringwood, Victoria, Australia
Penguin Books Canada Ltd, 2801 John Street, Markham, Ontario, Canada L3R 1B4
Penguin Books (N.Z.) Ltd, 182–190 Wairau Road, Auckland 10, New Zealand

—

First published 1981

—

Copyright © H. Golombek, 1981

All rights reserved

—

Made and printed in Great Britain
by Richard Clay (The Chaucer Press) Ltd,
Bungay, Suffolk
Set in Monotype Times

# CONTENTS

# INTRODUCTION

Chess is an easy game to learn but a difficult one to master, and this makes it an ideal hobby for those who like to exercise their wits. When I say it is difficult to become a master of the game I do not at all mean that you have to be a mastermind to play the game well. I have known one real mathematical genius in my life and he, while passionately fond of chess, played it atrociously. I could give him the odds of a Queen (the most powerful piece in the game) and still beat him. No, all you need is the average intelligence of an ordinary human being.

Another fortunate circumstance is that it is not an expensive hobby. Great sums of money are not involved, nor should you imagine that if you become a good chess-player you are going to enrich your bank account. Only perhaps if you have ambitions for the world championship title . . .

Chess does indeed have some therapeutic value in the matter of training the mind; it helps to concentrate the mind wonderfully. But so, according to Dr Johnson, does the prospect of being hanged next day.

The chief reward you will get from learning to play chess is the sheer fun and enjoyment you will derive from playing a game which is full of colourful ideas and sudden vicissitudes. It has been entrancing mankind (and womankind too) for some 1,500 years and looks like doing the same for another 1,500.

Harry Golombek
Chalfont St Giles, 1979

# CHAPTER 1

# THE CHESS-BOARD AND THE CHESS-MEN

The game of chess is essentially a game between two players who oppose each other on the opposite sides of a chess-board which is square in shape. The board itself is made up of sixty-four small squares which are coloured alternately white and black. Though for the sake of convenience one terms these colours white and black, in practice the colours are usually better defined as light and dark, since the white is often a cream or yellow colour or even red (though this is mostly seen in oriental sets), whilst the black can be any dark shade of brown and is, when black, of varying degrees of blackness, ranging from dull to ebony.

The chess-board is placed between the two players in such a way that the right-hand square of the bottom row of squares (i.e. the row nearest to each player) is white in colour as in Diagram 1.

Each horizontal row, usually termed 'rank', and each vertical

1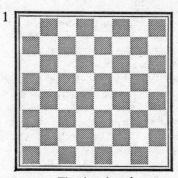

The chess-board

row, usually called 'file', consists of eight squares with the alter-
nation in colour already mentioned. Each player possesses enough
pieces to fill the first two ranks and, since only one piece can
occupy one square, each player has an army numbering sixteen
pieces.

I have used the word 'army' deliberately since chess was in
origin a war game and may still be regarded as a war or struggle
between two States. In view of this, it is entirely fitting that the
more important pieces should be in the rear, on the back rank,
and that the cannon-fodder, the infantry, should be placed in the
front, on the second rank.

Here is the initial position of the pieces.

2

The original set-up

Each player has eight pawns on his second rank, the word 'pawn'
having originally meant 'foot-soldier'. The pieces on the back
rank, looking at them from left to right, are Rook, Knight,
Bishop, Queen, King, Bishop, Knight and Rook. These eight
pieces represent the power and might of a medieval State. (At that
time the Rook was known as a Castle, as it has been right up to
the twentieth century; though in origin, some 1,500 years ago, it
was in fact a different war-weapon – a chariot.) For many years
now it has been represented by a tower or turret, as can be seen
by the French word for the piece: *tour*, meaning tower.

A good way of remembering the relative initial position of King and Queen is to bear in mind that the Queen is placed initially on a square of its own colour, that is, the White Queen on a white square and the Black Queen on a black square, and that the King is initially placed on a square of opposite colour, that is, the White King is on a black-coloured square and the Black King is on a white-coloured square.

One player has the White men and the other has the Black. For the sake of representing this in diagrammatic form we always put the White pieces at the bottom of a diagram and the Black pieces at the top. The player who has the White pieces moves first, then Black makes his reply to which White replies, and so on, play proceeding by alternate moves till the end of the game. It is in fact a slight advantage to have White since White, being the first to move, is to that extent ahead of his opponent. Hence, when one has White one should be concerned with the processes of attack; as Black one should be concentrating on defence.

Though the King is the most important piece on the board it is one of the weakest in power and its field of action is limited to one square in any direction. Thus, as can be seen in Diagram 3, it moves only one square, vertically or horizontally or diagonally: that is to say, it can go forward one square, backward one square,

3

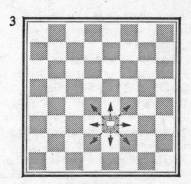

The King's move

sideways one square or diagonally one square. Naturally, it cannot go in all directions at once but must limit itself to one of these directions.

Since pieces capture enemy pieces by moving on to the square occupied by the enemy piece, the King can capture an enemy by moving its one square. Thus, in Diagram 4, the White King can capture the enemy (Black) pawn by moving one square forward, or it can capture the Bishop by moving one square back or the Knight by moving one square diagonally.

4

How the King captures

The King cannot capture the enemy King; likewise, it cannot be captured by its opposite number. Moreover, it cannot move to a square adjacent to the enemy King, so that there must always be at least one square in between the two Kings. Thus, in Diagram 5, the White King cannot move one square forward. Similarly, the Black King, if it is Black's turn to move, also cannot move one square forward.

Finally, the King may not move to a square on which it is attacked by an enemy piece, a prohibition which, as we shall see later on, does not apply to the other pieces.

All these rules really relate to the vital importance of the King; and Shakespeare's line in *Hamlet* 'There's such divinity doth hedge a King' could very well be applied to a chess King.

Next in importance to the King is the Queen which, as you can see if you look at Diagram 2, starts off the game on the square next to the King. The two monarchs in fact jointly occupy the centre of the first rank.

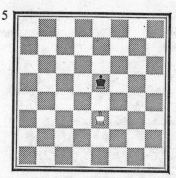

King cannot touch King

The Queen is also the strongest piece on the board, by which I mean that it is the most far-ranging piece and the one that controls the greatest number of squares. It can move along the rank, along the file and along the diagonal and, always providing there is no piece in the way, it can move right to the edge of the board.

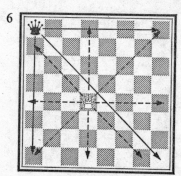

The Queen's move

13

Here you will see that the Queen governs twenty-seven squares when it is placed in the centre and twenty-one when it is in a corner. No other piece has anything like this field of action and indeed the King, with its eight possible squares, presents a feeble contrast.

Note that both the Queen and the King have crowns but that the King usually possesses a bigger, taller crown and that of the Queen is shallower and resembles a coronet in that it has a serrated edge. A good tip by which you can make sure of having the King and the Queen in their right place at the beginning of the game is this: the Queen should be on the square of its own colour and the King should be on the square of the colour of the opposing King. Thus a White Queen should start off the game on a white square and a Black Queen should be on a black square; a White King should be on a black square and a Black King on a white square. Naturally, these are all starting points and, once the game has begun, both the Queen and King are at liberty to go to a square of either colour.

Directly adjacent to the Queen on the left and to the King on the right are the two Bishops. They can only move diagonally and in consequence can never leave the colour of the square on which they find themselves initially. The maximum number of squares a Bishop can traverse is thirteen and this even applies to

7
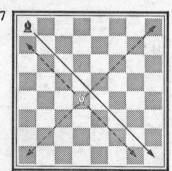

The Bishop's move

14

the piece when it is centrally placed, as the White Bishop is in Diagram 7. When it is in a corner (this also appears in Diagram 7) it only commands seven squares. This means it is more powerful when it is placed in the centre, and as a general rule you should aim at placing it there. The outward characteristic of the Bishop is the mitre the piece wears on its head, this being usually represented by a pointed cap with a cleft in the middle.

Both Queen and Bishop capture by occupying the square of the enemy, as in Diagram 8 where the White Queen can capture the Black pawn by advancing to the square on which the pawn stands and the Black Bishop can capture the White pawn by doing likewise. Note that neither piece can go through the square on which an enemy stands: the furthest each can go is by capturing it (removing it from the board) and occupying the square on which it stands.

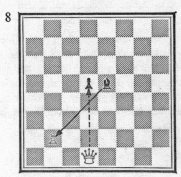

How the Queen and Bishop
capture

Next to the Bishops come the Knights, which usually appear as horses' heads, this being a relic of their role as cavalry in the game when it was invented, some 1,500 years ago. The Knight has a method of moving that is really a combination of two types of move. It goes two squares along a rank and then one square along a file, or it may go two squares along a file and then one

15

square along a rank. Thus, in Diagram 9, the various possible Knight moves form a sort of wheel. When placed in the centre, it has a scope of sixteen squares, but when in the corner (as can also be seen in Diagram 9) it has only six squares. Even these

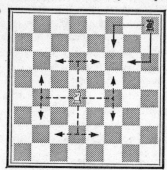

The Knight's move

figures are, in one sense, exaggerated since (unlike the Bishop, Queen or Rook) it cannot stop short of its maximum movement, but must go the full two squares and then the one square. So one might say in amendment that when placed in the centre it commands eight squares, and when in the corner only two.

But the Knight has another advantage in the way it moves

The Knight's leap

which it owes to its origin as cavalry: it can leap over anything in its path, whether what is in the way be friend or foe. Thus, in Diagram 10, the White Knight can leap over the Black pawn or the White pawn or the Black Queen or the Black Bishop. All beginners find this method of moving so mysterious that they overestimate the powers of the Knight which are, after all, inferior to those at the command of its nearest rival, the Bishop, especially in an open board (that is, one denuded of pieces). It is worth while practising the Knight's move quite a lot at this stage so as to get accustomed to its strange way of moving.

The Rooks, which initially stand on the corner squares of the board, are powerful pieces with a sweep, on their original square, of seven squares along the entire file or along the entire rank. They stand next to the Queen in power but, unlike the Queen, are unable to move diagonally. Like the other pieces, they capture by occupying the square on which the enemy piece is placed. Both the move and the method of capture are illustrated in Diagram 11.

11

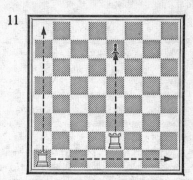

The Rook's move and its
method of capture

The Rook on the second rank can move forward as far as the seventh rank; there it occupies the square on which the pawn stands and, in so doing, captures it and removes it from the board.

These are the moves of all the pieces on the first rank. On the second rank there are eight pawns, all rather nondescript in shape, as befits the humble nature of the pawn which was originally a foot-soldier. The pawn's normal move is one square forwards; but, on its first move in the game, each pawn can move one square or two squares, according to the wishes of the player. It cannot move backwards and its only method of capture is diagonally. The moves and the method of capture are shown in Diagram 12.

12

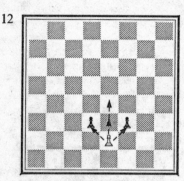

The pawn's move and its
method of capture

Here the White pawn has five possibilities to choose from: it can take off the pawn on the file to its left; or it can capture the pawn on the right; or it can advance one square; or it can advance two squares; or it need not move at all.

There is one other move that is vital to the course of the game, and it concerns the King. You will remember that I said that the King cannot capture another King. It is also true that the King is not to be taken by any piece. However, the King cannot move into a position where it is attacked by any enemy piece. On the other hand any enemy piece may attack the King – this is known as checking the King. When one side checks the other side it is imperative for the side so checked to get away from the check immediately. This can be done either by capturing the checking piece, or by interposing one's own piece, or by moving away from the check. In Diagram 13 all the white pieces can, if they like, check the King. Naturally, only one of them can give check at a time, but if White wants to give check with the Queen he has four different possible ways of so doing: he may move the Queen to the eighth rank and so check the King horizontally; he may check

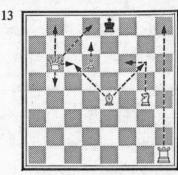

13

Check!

the King on the diagonal by moving the Queen one square to the right; he may check the King on the diagonal by moving the Queen one square back; and finally he may give check by moving the Queen diagonally to the square adjacent to the King (though he would be unwise to make this last move, since then Black could reply by simply taking off the Queen with his King). The White pawn may give check by moving one square forward and thus attack the King diagonally. The White Bishop may check the King in one of two ways: either by advancing diagonally to the right, or by advancing diagonally to the left (in both cases it must move two squares). The Knight can check the King by advancing two squares vertically and then moving one square to the left, horizontally. And finally the Rook can check the King by moving to the end of the file.

This description of the moves of all the pieces comprises the basic moves and, as you can see, they are not particularly complicated. There are indeed some more complicated ones, and these I have left to Chapter 4. It is a good idea at this stage for you to try out the moves I have already described over the chessboard, preferably with someone else sitting opposite you on the other side of the board. But, if there is no one else to hand, you can still get the feel of the pieces and become accustomed to moving them by trying them out yourself alone on the chessboard.

A word of warning as to the set of chess-men you should use: do not go in for anything fancy or particularly artistic. Colourful or beautiful sets usually indulge in a certain amount of fantasy as regards the portrayal of the pieces, and you may well find you are unable to distinguish between the various kinds of pieces. In any case, if your set is of great value and rarity, consider the tragedy if one of the pieces is lost. No, get yourself a sound, solid-looking set of what is known as the Staunton pattern, after the great British nineteenth-century player, Howard Staunton.

## EXERCISES

14

1. What is wrong with the way the pieces are set out in this position?

15

2. What is wrong with the way the pieces are set out in this position?

16

3. Whose turn is it to move, White's or Black's?

17

4. Where, if it is White's turn to move, can his King go? How many different moves can (a) the White Bishop, (b) the White Knight and (c) the White Rook make? Where, if it is Black's turn to move, can the Black King go? How many different moves can (a) the Black Queen, (b) the Black pawn and (c) the Black Rook make?

18

5. Can the White Knight move and, if so, to how many different squares? How many different ways, if any, can it attack the enemy King?

19

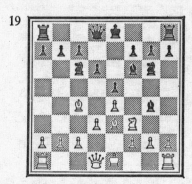

6. What is wrong with this position?

20

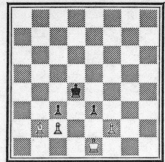

7. With White to play, how can his pawns move? With Black to play, how can his pawns move?

21

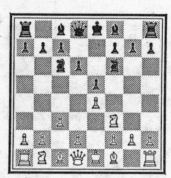

8. White to play: how can the Bishops move? With Black to play, how can the Black Bishops move? With White to play, it might seem that Black has made one more move than White, if you count the number of moves made on the board by each side. But this is impossible since in fact White always starts play. What then is the explanation?

## ANSWERS TO THE EXERCISES

**1.** (see Diagram 14) The chess-board is the wrong way round. It should always be set up with a white square on the extreme right-hand of the first rank. Since this has not been done in Exercise 1, you will find the Kings are on the same colour square as their own and that the Queens are on the opposite colour square to their own. But this is in fact the reverse of what should happen. You can always tell that you have got the board set correctly if the Queens are initially placed on the same colour square as their own, i.e. when the White Queen is on a white square and the Black Queen on a black square. Similarly, you have got the board the right way round when the White King is initially on a black square and the Black King is initially on a white square.

**2.** (see Diagram 15) If you look at the first rank, you will find that the White Knight on the right-hand side is where the White Bishop should be, and vice versa. The other thing that is wrong with the position is that the Black King and the Black Queen are occupying each other's square. Remember that the Queen should be on a square of its own colour while the King should be on the opposite-coloured square.

**3.** (see Diagram 16) It should be, normally, White's turn to move. White makes the first move in the game and, if he has started off by advancing his pawn two squares, as he is perfectly entitled to do when he first moves the pawn, then Black must have done likewise. Only in the remote possibility of White having played his pawn up one square on his first move and, with Black replying by pushing up his pawn two squares, then advancing it yet again another single square, would we find that it was Black's turn to move.

**4.** (see Diagram 17) With White to move, his King can move one square to the right along the rank.

The White Bishop can make nine different moves. Moving

along the diagonal (remember it can only move on a diagonal), it can advance upwards to the right to any one of four squares. Alternatively, moving along the same diagonal but this time downwards to the left, it can go two squares. Moving diagonally to the left it can advance upwards two squares or, on the same diagonal but this time downwards to the right, it can go one square where, at the same time, it checks the opposing King.

The White Knight can make any one of four moves: it can move to the square directly below the White King; it can go to the square directly above the White King; it can move to the square directly on the right of the Black King; or, finally, it can advance to the right-hand square of the rank on which the enemy King is stationed.

The White Rook has fourteen moves at its disposal: it can move vertically upwards for three squares, downwards for four and horizontally another seven.

With Black to move, the Black King can only go one square to the left.

The Black Queen can make fourteen different moves: it can move along six squares of the bottom rank and seven squares of the vertical file. It can also make one move diagonally.

The Black pawn can make only one move–forward to the next square vertically.

The Black Rook can make six moves along the rank and four moves vertically – ten moves in all.

5. (see Diagram 18) Since the Knight has the capacity for jumping over other pieces it can certainly move, and that to eight different squares. It can attack the enemy King in one of two ways: either by moving two squares to the left along the rank and then one square downwards vertically, or by moving two squares upwards vertically and then one square laterally to the right.

6. (see Diagram 19) Nothing is wrong with this position. True, at first glance it might seem that the position of the Black Bishop and the Black Knight on the right-hand side of the diagram should be interchanged, since normally the Knight moves to the

square on which the Black Bishop stands in the diagram and the Bishop moves along the diagonal of its original square.

But the Bishop might well have been brought to its position on the third rank by advancing it one square diagonally on its first move then one square diagonally on its second move. The Black Knight too might have been brought to its present position by being played first of all to the square in front of the King and then, on the next move, to its position in the diagram.

7. (see Diagram 20) The White pawn on the third file cannot move at all, but the other White pawn, the one on the sixth file (counting from left to right), can make three different moves: it can capture the Black pawn, giving check to the King at the same time; it can move one square forward; or, since this is its initial move, it can move two squares forward.

With Black to play, he has, like White, three possible pawn moves. His pawn on the third file, like White's, cannot move forward, but it can capture the White Bishop. Black's other pawn, that on the fifth file (counting from left to right), has two possible moves: it can move one square forward or it can take the White pawn with check.

8. (see Diagram 21) With White to play, the Bishop on the left, three squares along, has no moves since it is hemmed in by its own pawns. But the Bishop on the right can move along any one of the five squares on the diagonal which has been opened up for it by the advance of the King's pawn. Naturally, it would be committing suicide if it did in fact advance the full length of the diagonal; so, in practical terms, it has only four squares along which it can reasonably travel.

With Black to play, both Bishops can move, since both the centre Black pawns have been advanced, allowing the Bishops diagonals along which to move. The Bishop next to the King can move only one square along the diagonal since all further progress is prevented by the Black Queen's pawn. But the other Bishop, that next to the Queen, can make five moves along the diagonal open to it. As in the case of the White Bishop mentioned in the previous paragraph, it would be suicidal folly to move it to the full length of the diagonal, since there it would be captured by the White pawn.

The explanation as to why Black seems to have made one more move than White is that White has taken two moves to get his King's pawn advanced to the centre, whereas Black has taken only one.

# CHAPTER 2

# CHESS NOTATION; THE OBJECT OF
# THE GAME AND THE SIMPLER MATES

Chess is a fortunate game in that, unlike most other games, it is possible to keep a full and clear record of its progress so that all games played on the chess-board can be recorded in a simple notation and replayed later if so desired. In earlier times, five hundred or more years ago, games were indeed recorded but only in very lengthy and tedious fashion: for example, if the pawn in front of the King was moved, the moving would be described as 'the King's pawn advances to the third square of its file'.

Such a notation was a slow method of describing a slow game; but for modern chess a much more concise and speedy notation was required and invented. In the descriptive notation which is largely used in English- and Spanish-speaking countries, the move described at the end of the previous paragraph is represented by just four symbols. But the basis of the description remains the same in that the chess-men and the squares on the chess-board are represented by the initials of the pieces and the positions of these pieces on the chess-board at the beginning of the game.

With the one exception of the Knight, each piece is represented by its initial letter. Thus K = King, Q = Queen, B = Bishop, R = Rook and P = Pawn. The Knight used to be represented by Kt in order to distinguish it from K for King; but this has become a little old-fashioned and more common nowadays is N for Knight, a practice that was introduced to this country from the U.S.A. Though a mis-spelling as far as the English language is concerned, it has the merit of brevity and is, at any rate, phonetically correct.

The squares on the chess-board are numbered from 1 to 8 up the file, and in Diagram 22 the number and name of each square

are shown, looking at the position from White's point of view, i.e. with White playing up the board.

Note that where there are a pair of pieces of the same kind (Rooks, Knights and Bishops) the squares on which they are initially placed are distinguished by the addition of Q or K,

22

| QR8 | QN8 | QB8 | Q8 | K8 | KB8 | KN8 | KR8 |
| QR7 | QN7 | QB7 | Q7 | K7 | KB7 | KN7 | KR7 |
| QR6 | QN6 | QB6 | Q6 | K6 | KB6 | KN6 | KR6 |
| QR5 | QN5 | QB5 | Q5 | K5 | KB5 | KN5 | KR5 |
| QR4 | QN4 | QB4 | Q4 | K4 | KB4 | KN4 | KR4 |
| QR3 | QN3 | QB3 | Q3 | K3 | KB3 | KN3 | KR3 |
| QR2 | QN2 | QB2 | Q2 | K2 | KB2 | KN2 | KR2 |
| QR1 | QN1 | QB1 | Q1 | K1 | KB1 | KN1 | KR1 |

according to whether they are nearer the Queen or the King. This distinction is vitally important to the whole system since otherwise one would not be able to tell which piece moved to which square. For example, in Diagram 23, the White Knight on the King-side (i.e. on the side of the board nearer the King) is placed

23

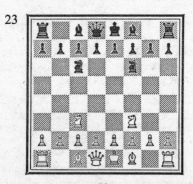

on KB3 and, similarly, the White Knight on the Queen-side is placed on QB3.

The actual process of moving a piece is represented by a horizontal dash (–), and the whole move is described by the symbol for the piece that is moved, followed by a dash, then the name and number of the square to which the piece is moved. Thus, in Diagram 23, the move of the White Knight on the King-side is indicated by N–KB3 and that of the other White Knight by N–QB3. We also put down the number of the move made. So, if it was the King's Knight that moved first in Diagram 23, then it would be described as *1*. N–KB3, and if, after Black had moved his Knight in reply, White had proceeded to move his second Knight (as he has done in Diagram 23), then that is shown as *2*. N–B3. Observe that we no longer have to add the full name of the square on to which the QN moves. For the first Knight has already gone to KB3 and there is only one square for White left to be called B3. This principle of economy is followed throughout the game with the descriptive system of notation and it does save quite a number of symbols.

A capture is indicated by a ×. Thus, if in Diagram 23, White, whose turn it is to move, plays *3*. P–QN4, Black may reply *3*. ..., N × P. Note that you do not have to write *3*. ..., QN × QNP as there is only one pawn that can be taken and only one specific Knight that can do the capturing.

However, if the game shown in the last diagram had proceeded further to the position in Diagram 24, then *5*. N × P, would be ambiguous and incorrect. If the Knight had taken off the QP then the move would rightly read *5*. N × QP; but if, on the other hand, it had captured the QNP, then the right term for the move would be *5*. N × NP. Again, we do not need to say *5*. N × QNP, since there is only one NP within the range of the Knight.

Similarly if, instead of moving the Knight, White had played *5*. B × P, there would have been no need to add to the symbols with *5*. B × QNP, or, still more absurdly, *5*. KB × QNP.

The process of giving check is indicated by the first two letters of the word, ch. Thus, with the game now having got as far as the position in Diagram 25, White proceeds to capture the Knight with his Bishop, and that move is shown as *6. B × N ch.*

But White has a number of other moves at his disposal in the

24

game as shown in Diagram 25. He need not play *6. B × N ch,* but can, if he so likes, make a composite move, a joint move with his King and Rook that is called Castling. This consists of

25

moving the King two squares to the right and simultaneously bringing the Rook two squares to the left. This process, which is aimed at bringing the King into a safe position in the corner of the board, would appear here as *6. O – O,* and then the position would appear as in Diagram 26.

You can only castle when the squares between the King and the Rook are vacant. You cannot castle the King into a position in which it is in check. This is because the rules state that the

26

King cannot move into a position where it is checked by the enemy. The same rules also state that you cannot castle out of check, nor can you, in castling, move the King across a square which is attacked by an enemy piece.

This is castling with the KR; but one can also castle with the QR and this Queen-side castling is indicated by adding a third O. Thus, taking the position in Diagram 26 one stage further, so that we now have that in Diagram 27 where we have a clear run

27

between the Black King and his QR, after White has played 7. Q–K2, then Black may play 7. . . ., O–O–O and the position is as shown in Diagram 28.

28

In Diagram 29 each King is in a position to castle King-side (O–O) or Queen-side (O–O–O) according to his wish. The various paths that could be followed are shown. Note that whereas in King-side castling the King and the Rook both travel two squares, in Queen-side castling the King travels two squares but the Rook travels three squares.

As regards notation, I have been looking at the board till now from the White point of view. But both White and Black have a

29

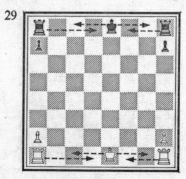

point of view and this means that the numbers of the squares are reversed when one looks at the board from the Black point of view, as is shown in Diagram 30.

30

| QR1 | QN1 | QB1 | Q1 | K1 | KB1 | KN1 | KR1 |
|------|------|------|------|------|------|------|------|
| QR2 | QN2 | QB2 | Q2 | K2 | KB2 | KN2 | KR2 |
| QR3 | QN3 | QB3 | Q3 | K3 | KB3 | KN3 | KR3 |
| QR4 | QN4 | QB4 | Q4 | K4 | KB4 | KN4 | KR4 |
| QR5 | QN5 | QB5 | Q5 | K5 | KB5 | KN5 | KR5 |
| QR6 | QN6 | QB6 | Q6 | K6 | KB6 | KN6 | KR6 |
| QR7 | QN7 | QB7 | Q7 | K7 | KB7 | KN7 | KR7 |
| QR8 | QN8 | QB8 | Q8 | K8 | KB8 | KN8 | KR8 |

To illustrate how a whole game appears in this notation I give a short game that occurred in the Clare Benedict International Team Tournament at Middlesbrough, 1979.

WHITE: ROBATSCH      BLACK: HVENEKILDE
(AUSTRIA)         (DENMARK)

*1.* P–QB4

White's first move was pawn from the QB2 square to the QB4 square. Note that he has exercised his right to move his pawn two squares since this was the pawn's first move.

*1.* ...             N–KB3

Black replies to White's first move by moving his Knight from the KN1 square to the KB3 square. Note that if you had put down here N–B3 this would be ambiguous, since either Knight could go to B3 (either to KB3 or to QB3). Also note that when Black moves, the notation is made from the Black point of view (see Diagram 30).

*2.* N–QB3

The White Knight from QN1 (the Queen's Knight) goes to the square QB3. Again, just N–B3 would have been ambiguous, since the Knight could have then gone to either QB3 or KB3.

2.  ...                              P–K3

The Black pawn on K2 goes to the square K3. Also quite playable would have been advancing this pawn two squares, i.e. P–K4.

3. N–B3

White's King's Knight goes from the square KN1 to the square KB3. It is no longer necessary to put the move in full as N–KB3, since the other Knight has already gone to QB3.

3.  ...                              P–Q4

The Black pawn goes from the Q2 square to the Q4 square.

4. P–Q4

White's Queen's pawn advances two squares to its Q4 square.

4.  ...                              B–K2

The Black Bishop moves from the KB1 square to the K2 square (its shortest possible move).

5. B–B4

The White Bishop goes from QB1 to the KB4 square. No need to say B–KB4 or QB–B4 since there is only one Bishop that can go to White's KB4.

5.  ...                              O–O

Black's King castles with Black's Rook, i.e. the Black King moves two squares along the rank and the Black King's Rook does likewise, the two pieces passing over each other.

6. P–K3

White King's pawn advances one square to the K3 square.

6.  ...                              R–K1

The Black Rook moves from the KB square to the K1 square.

7. R–B1

The White Rook on the QR1 square goes to the QB1 square.

      7. ...                                 P–QR3

The Black pawn on the QR2 square advances one square to QR3. Note that it is necessary to specify to which R3 the pawn goes, as otherwise it might be the KR3 square.

      8. P–QR3

The White pawn on QR2 goes to the QR3 square. The same note as that to Black's seventh move applies here.

      8. ...                                 P–B3

The Black pawn on the QB2 square goes to the QB3 square. It is not necessary to say QB3 in the notation, since this is the only pawn that can advance on a Bishop file.

      9. B–Q3

The White Bishop on the KB1 square goes to the Q3 square.

      9. ...                               QN–Q2

The Knight on the QN1 square goes to the Q2 square. It is necessary to say QN, since otherwise the KN might go to Q2.

      10. P–B5

The pawn on QB4 goes to QB5. P–B5, however, is enough, since the KB pawn cannot go to B5.

      10. ...                             P–QN3

The Black pawn on the QN2 square advances one square to the QN3 square. Note that P–N3 would be ambiguous and that it is therefore necessary to specify which N3 is meant.

      11. P × P

The White pawn on the QB5 square takes the Black pawn on the QN6 square.

      11. ...                             P–B4?

The Black pawn on the QB3 square advances one square to the

QB4 square. The question mark after the move means that it is a bad move; this is the normal short way of expressing disapproval of a move. Had it been a good move, I would have expressed it by the addition of an exclamation mark (by P–B4!).

*12.* B–B7                                    resigns.

The White Bishop on the KB4 square goes to the QB7 square and Black, seeing that he must lose his very valuable Queen for the White Bishop (which is worth much less), decides that his position is hopeless and therefore resigns.

The final position in which Black resigns is shown in Diagram 31.

31

The object of the game of chess, like all games, is to win. But the basic and specific objective of chess is to deliver 'checkmate' to the adversary: this means to render the King of the opponent so helpless that, no matter what move he makes, he cannot avoid his King being captured. There are many ways of doing this but all involve a narrowing-down of the attack on the enemy King very much as a hunter pursues his prey. You allow him less and less scope for escape and then you make a swoop on him in a way that shows the inevitability of capture. A simple example of this final swoop is shown in Diagram 32.

Now White plays *1.* R–Q8 and this is checkmate since, no

32

matter what the Black King now tries to do, he cannot escape from capture by the Rook.

This is a mate along the rank (one can and often does use 'mate' instead of the longer word, checkmate) and so you could call it a horizontal mate; a mate along the file (a vertical mate) can also be achieved by a Rook move, as in Diagram 33. Here White plays *1.* R–QR2, which is checkmate.

33

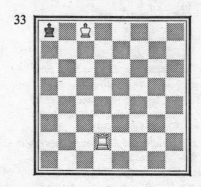

Similar mates can be given by the Queen, but this piece can also mate along the diagonal, as in Diagram 34. Here White mates by *1.* Q–Q5.

39

34

Mate along the diagonal can also be achieved by the Bishop. Here White plays *1*. B–Q5 and it is checkmate.

35

Even the lowly pawn, feeble though it is by contrast with the other pieces, can give mate on the diagonal, since its only method of capturing is of course along the diagonal. In Diagram 36, White plays *1*. PN–7 and it is checkmate.

Nor is the Knight without checkmating powers. In Diagram 37, White plays *1*. N–B6, checkmate.

All these examples show the winner on the point of delivering the *coup de grâce*. But how does one arrive at such positions? Well, sometimes it is not even necessary to progress to the actual checkmate; the game I gave earlier in this chapter was an example of a win which never even bordered on the checkmating position,

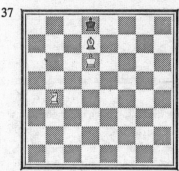

for in it Black satisfied himself that eventually White would reach a position where he could force checkmate.

But if it is necessary to force a checkmate then, of course, it is also necessary to know how to force a checkmate. The simplest set-up that will enable you to force checkmate is that in which you have two Rooks against a bare and solitary King (Diagram 38).

White starts the narrowing-down process by playing *1.* R–R4. Then comes

        *1.* ...                             K–K4

Black tries to give himself as much space as possible; but now White forces the enemy King back with

       *2.* R–B5 ch

41

38

Black does his best to counter-attack with

    *2.* ...                           K–Q3

And White must spend a move putting his Rook into safety.

    *3.* R–QR5

Again Black tries to get near to and attack an enemy Rook with

    *3.* ...                            K–B3

And White checks him back to the second rank with

    *4.* R–KR6 ch             K–N2

Whereupon White must spend a move putting his Rook where it can check the King from a distance, but the end is near.

    *5.* R–N5

We need not specify which N5 this is, since R–QN5 would be with check, and the notation would read R–N5 ch.

    Black tries to get into the open as much as possible with

    *5.* ...                            K–B2

But White now delivers checkmate in two moves.

    *6.* R–N7 ch             K–Q1 (or B1 or N1)
    *7.* R–R8 checkmate.

Observe that when you have two Rooks against a bare King you do not need to use your own King but can deliver mate quite easily without bringing your King into action. When, however, you have King and Queen against the bare King, you cannot force mate without using your King as well as the Queen. Thus, in the position in Diagram 39, your best method of forcing mate is to make use of your King to help drive the enemy King back.

39

| 1. K–B3 | K–B4 |

If the Black King goes anywhere else, either to B3 or Q3, then White advances with his King to B4.

| 2. Q–K5 ch | K–B3 |
| 3. K–B4 | K–N3 |
| 4. Q–Q6 ch | |

All the time White is beating back the enemy King and narrowing down the space at its disposal.

| 4. ... | K–N2 |
| 5. K–N5 | |

40

Now Black can make one of three moves:

*Line 1*

|  |  |
|---|---|
| 5. ... | K–R2 |
| 6. Q–Q7 ch | K–N1 |
| 7. K–N6 | |

White would have made the same move if Black had played 6. ..., K–R1.

|  |  |
|---|---|
| 7. ... | K–R1 |
| 8. Q–QN7 checkmate. | |

Now go back to the position in Diagram 40.

*Line 2*

|  |  |
|---|---|
| 5. ... | K–B1 |
| 6. Q–K7 | |

Confining the Black King to the back rank.

|  |  |
|---|---|
| 6. ... | K–N1 |
| 7. K–N6 | K–B1 |
| 8. Q–QB7 checkmate. | |

If Black had played 7. ..., K–R1 then White mates by 8. Q–QN7 or by 8. Q–QR7 or by 8. Q–Q8 or by moving the Queen to anywhere on the eighth rank.

Once again, go back to Diagram 40.

*Line 3*

|  |  |
|---|---|
| 5. ... | K–R1 |
| 6. Q–Q7 | |

Once again confining the Black King to the back rank.

|  |  |
|---|---|
| 6. ... | K–N1 |

And White checkmates by the same process as in Line 1.

|  |  |
|---|---|
| 7. K–N6 | K–R1 |
| 8. Q–QN7 checkmate. | |

This type of mate is also an easy one, only slightly more difficult than that with two Rooks, since the Queen is the equivalent in strength of two Rooks.

### EXERCISES

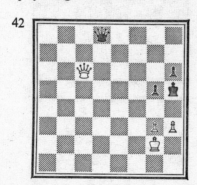

41

1. White to play and give checkmate in one move.

42

2. White to play and checkmate in two moves.

43

**3.** White to play and checkmate in one move.

44

**4.** White to play and checkmate in one move.

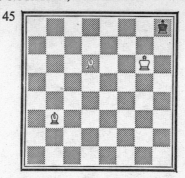

5.  White to play and checkmate in one move.

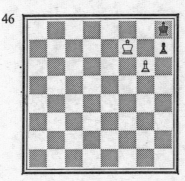

6.  White to play and checkmate in one move.

47

7. White to play and checkmate in one move.

48

8. White to play and checkmate in three moves.

49

9. White to play and force checkmate in, at most, four moves.

### ANSWERS TO THE EXERCISES

1. (see Diagram 41) White mates in one move on the diagonal by *1*. Q–K8. He can also mate on the file by *1*. P–N4 ch, K–R5 ; *2*. Q × P mate, but this would take one move longer. Note that the check by *1*. Q–B3 ch, would be bad since it would allow the King to escape from the mating net by *1*. . . ., K–N3.

2. (see Diagram 42) White mates in two moves along the file by *1*. P–N4 ch, K–R5; *2*. Q × P mate. Again, checking on B3 would allow the enemy King to escape on N3.

3. (see Diagram 43) White mates in one move along the rank by *1*. R–B8 mate.

4. (see Diagram 44) White gives mate along the file by *1*. R–R2 mate.

5. (see Diagram 45) White mates with the Bishop along the diagonal by *1*. B–K5 mate.

6. (see Diagram 46) White mates with the pawn along the diagonal by *1*. P–N7 mate.

7. (see Diagram 47) White mates with the Knight by *1*. N–N6 checkmate. Note that after the other possible check *1*. N–B7 ch?, Black's King could escape by *1*. . . ., K–N1.

8. (see Diagram 48) White mates in three moves by *1*. R–B6 ch, K–B2; *2*. R–N7 ch, K–Q1; *3*. R–B8 checkmate.

9. (see Diagram 49) White starts off the mating process by *1*. K–B5, since in this ending it is essential to use the King as well as the Queen so as to enforce mate. The King move has considerably limited Black's possible lines and he has now to choose between two moves: (A) *1*. ..., K–B1; *2*. K–N6, K–N1; *3*. Q–K8 or *3*. Q–N7, in both cases with checkmate; or (B) *1*. ..., K–N1; *2*. Q–K7, K–R1; *3*. K–N6, K–N1; and again either *4*. Q–K8 or *4*. Q–N7 is checkmate.

This is only a small sample of the many kinds of fairly obvious checkmates that you can obtain. A good plan for practising checkmates is to set up various positions on the board that you think might lead to a speedy checkmate, and then try and work out how in fact this would be done.

# CHAPTER 3

# OTHER OBJECTIVES – THE DRAWN GAME

We have seen that the main ambition in the game must lie in beating the adversary and either delivering checkmate or else forcing him to realize that his plight is hopeless and that the best way for him to end his misery is to resign. In such cases you score a point for your team, if you are playing in a team match, or for yourself if playing in a tournament. But there is also another possibility, the draw, which is a sort of compromise between winning and losing. It is therefore only natural that when you draw you score half a point, as indeed does the player with whom you draw.

How is this peaceful aim achieved? Well, in the first and commonest place, by agreement. One side will offer the draw and the other will accept the offer if he thinks he can do no better than draw. Normally this position will be such that the material is level, i.e. the pieces remaining to either side are about equal in value. There is also another circumstance that is important. Neither side must be so placed that he cannot prevent his opponent from winning much material or delivering checkmate.

Such a position appears in Diagram 50 where the material possessed by either side is in fact exactly equal. Given reasonable play by either side, there is no means of effecting a win either for Black or for White. Note that in this position the Queens have been exchanged, and this is in fact a circumstance that readily leads to a draw.

In such positions there is little chance of one side or the other checkmating his adversary, and all that will happen is that the players will go on exchanging pieces until, in the last resort, there are only Kings left on the board.

Another cause for the draw lies in the reduction of forces on the board by exchanges so that there is not sufficient material to achieve a checkmate. The most obvious of such states is when the players have exchanged off all the pieces and each is left with a bare King. By no power on earth can a win be effected in such

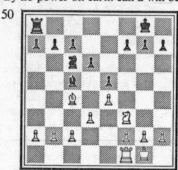

50

a case, and similarly a draw must be certain when the existing material is insufficient to force a checkmate, when, for example, each side is left with a solitary Bishop or a Knight. For you cannot give mate with a single Bishop or Knight.

Another kind of draw results when one player continually checks his opponent and the opponent cannot avoid this state of being continually in check. Such a state is known as perpetual check.

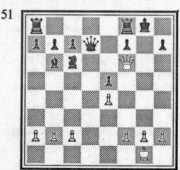

51

In this position White is obviously out-gunned by the enemy

since Black is no less than two Rooks, a Knight and a Bishop up on White. White therefore decides to force perpetual check by *1*. Q–N5 ch, K–R1; *2*. Q–B6 ch, K–N1; *3*. Q–N5 ch, etc.

If White tries to get more than the draw by, for instance, *1*. P–KR4 with the idea of playing this pawn to R6 so as to mate Black by Q–N7, then Black has time to consolidate his position by playing *1*. ..., Q–K3; and if then *2*. Q–N5 ch, Q–N3!

One of the more remarkable and fascinating types of draws is that known as stalemate, which arises when a player is on the move but has, however, no legal move at his disposal. In Diagram 52, with White to play, there is only one move by which White can retain his pawn, and that is *1*. K–K6. But, in retaining his pawn, White has prevented Black from moving his King and the game is a draw by stalemate.

52

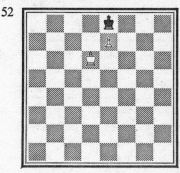

Stalemate can quite often occur when one player has a big advantage in material but carelessly overpushes this advantage, thereby allowing his opponent to escape with a draw. How this can occur can most clearly be seen if one considers the mating process with King and Queen versus King as described in the previous chapter. Go back to the position given in Diagram 40 where Black's King is on his QN2 and White's King is on QN5 and his Queen on Q6. The third line given on page 44 ran *5*. ..., K–R1; *6*. Q–Q7, etc. But suppose White had played *6*. Q–B7, when we would have got the position shown in Diagram

**53.** This is a stalemate in which White has carelessly thrown away the win. The moral is that, even when one is obviously winning, one should be on one's guard against inaccurate play. It is all too easy to throw away the fruits of previous good play through careless finishing tactics.

53

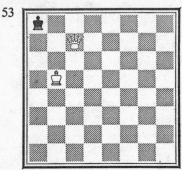

Stalemate is such an astonishing and brilliant device that it has given a new and most useful word to the English language. It is used most frequently by politicians and journalists to describe a temporary blockage. The number of times when negotiations aimed at settling a strike have reached stalemate in recent years must run into thousands. But it should be observed that, strictly speaking, its usage as indicating a temporary state of affairs is incorrect, since a stalemate in chess is permanent and constitutes the end of a game.

Perhaps the most complicated type of draw arises out of a repetition of position. In fact this kind of drawing process is another illustration of the perennial fascination of chess, since it is designed to eliminate any possible monotony in the game. Suppose, for example, a game was to drag on as follows: *1.* P–K4, P–K4; *2.* N–KB3, N–QB3; *3.* N–N1, N–N1; *4.* N–KB3, N–QB3; *5.* N–N1, N–N1; *6.* N–KB3, N–QB3 . . . etc. One would be forgiven for yawning with boredom at the 'etc.' process. Mercifully, if such a position appears three times with the same player having the move each time, then that player can claim a draw. The commonest type of draw by repetition of position occurs when one side has some advantage and is trying, in vain, to force it home to a win.

The draw by perpetual check could also be regarded as a variant of the draw by repetition of position, though not necessarily, since the checks might wander all over the board.

### EXERCISES

54

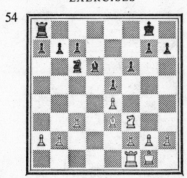

1. How should the game shown in this position end and, when it does end, what is the final result likely to be?

55

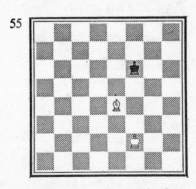

2. Can White hope to win in this position?

56

3. Black to play, what result and how?

57

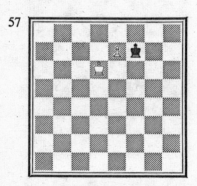

4. Black to play – how should he play in order to obtain a draw?

5.   Black to play – how can he obtain a draw by stalemate?

## ANSWERS TO THE EXERCISES

1. (see Diagram 54) This should end in a draw by agreement of the two players. The material is level as each side has a Rook, a Bishop, a Knight and seven pawns. Nor has either side an advantage in position.

2. (see Diagram 55) No, White cannot hope to win in this position since, no matter how indifferently his opponent plays, he cannot checkmate him.

3. (see Diagram 56) The game should end in a draw by perpetual check with *1.* ..., Q–N5 ch; *2.* K–R1, Q–B6 ch; *3.* K–N1, Q–N5 ch; etc.

4. (see Diagram 57) Black plays *1.* ..., K–K1; and White, if he wishes to save his pawn, must reply *2.* K–K6, after which the game is a draw by stalemate.

5. (see Diagram 58) Black looks to be in a bad way. White is threatening to checkmate him by playing his Queen to the eighth rank and if Black defends this by, say, *1.* ..., Q–K1; then White forces a win by playing *2.* Q–N6, advancing the RP to R7 and then playing Q–N8.

However, Black has an ingenious resource. He plays *1.* ..., Q–K3 ch; to which White must reply *2.* Q × Q, and the position is stalemate since the Black King cannot move.

## CHAPTER 4

# MORE MOVES AND ANOTHER NOTATION:
## THE ALGEBRAIC

When we talk about pieces in chess, we usually mean any piece which is of higher value than the humble, one-square-stepping pawn. For the pawn is indeed the feeblest force on the board. Even the King, which is so limited in its scope for action, is superior to the pawn in one important respect – it can move backwards.

However, this seemingly helpless unit is in fact the life-blood of the game and is potentially the strongest force on the board. This happens when the pawn reaches the eighth and last rank; it must then be promoted into a piece of the same colour, i.e. it must be exchanged for any one of the following four pieces: Bishop, Knight, Rook or Queen. It cannot remain as a pawn nor can it be promoted to a King; but when it gets to the eighth rank it must be changed into one of the four pieces I have mentioned.

In the position in Diagram 59, with White to play, he simply

59
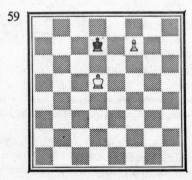

plays *1.* P–B8 = Q. The equals sign here means that White exchanges his pawn for a White Queen. Thereafter, as you can easily work out for yourself, it is a matter of mate in a few moves – to be precise, Black is mated in five more moves.

Push the Black King one square further back, as in Diagram 60. White can now promote his pawn into either a Queen or a Rook, and it is checkmate.

60

Curiously enough, positions occasionally occur in which it is imperative not to promote the pawn into the strongest possible piece.

61

In this position, if you play *1.* P–B8 = Q, you only get a draw by stalemate; whereas if you play *1.* P–B8 = R, Black is forced to reply *1. ...*, K–R3; whereupon you administer mate by *2*. R–R8. There are occasions where you may promote your pawn into a Queen or into a Bishop with exactly the same effect. Consider the position in Diagram 62 with White to play. Here you can play either *1*. P–B8 = Q or *1*. P–B8 = B, and in either case it is checkmate.

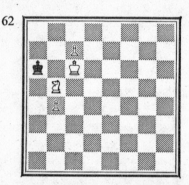

62

There are also times when you must promote the pawn into a Knight, and these also involve making your promotion with check. A neat little example would be as in Diagram 63. If White now plays *1*. P–B8 = Q, Black mates him in two moves by *1. ...*, Q–Q7 ch; *2*. K–N1, Q–N7.

63

Instead, you play *1*. P–B8 = N ch, and after *1*. ..., K–N2; *2*. N × Q ch, K–B3; *3*. P–R5, the White pawn cannot be stopped from Queening, and Black is quite lost.

Since the Knight works very well in co-operation with a Queen or a Rook to carry out a mating attack, there are also instances where it is advisable to promote the pawn to a Knight instead of a Queen in order to obtain just this type of mating attack.

64

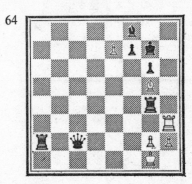

Here it would be worse than useless to promote the pawn to a Queen since Black would then administer checkmate on White's KN2. However, White can and does play *1*. P–K8 = N ch and Black must reply *1*. ..., K–N1; after which there follows *2*. N–B6 ch, K–N2; *3*. R–R7 mate. Note, by the way, that when one wants to indicate checkmate in a game score one usually abbreviates it to 'mate'.

Lest it should be thought I am exaggerating with these variations on the theme of promotion, let me tell you how my attempt to win the British Championship outright was once thwarted by the failure of a player to employ this possibility of promoting a pawn to a Knight. This was at Harrogate, 1947. I had finished my last-round game, having beaten the well-known Midlands expert B. H. Wood, the editor of *Chess*, and was leading with 8 points, half a point ahead of that fine player, R. J. Broadbent. I stayed to watch his game against R. H. Newman; if he won this game, then he won the championship; if he drew then we were level and would have to play off a match for the title; and if he lost, then I won the championship.

The game grew very exciting and suddenly I noticed that Newman could promote a pawn to a Knight, giving check and forcing a win. He did promote the pawn – but to a Queen; and after many complications the game was drawn. Afterwards I asked him why he hadn't made a Knight instead of a Queen: 'Never thought of it' was the reply. Well, if you have a similar situation, no doubt you will think of it.

## TAKING *EN PASSANT*

From what has been written about the pawn so far, it will be realized that there is more to the pawn than meets the eye. True, it starts off as a sort of foot-soldier, inferior to every other piece on the board. But, as the game goes on, so it increases in value and power. Its moves seem simple enough, and yet in the end great complicated schemes may be executed with the aid of the pawn.

There is, though, one move of the pawn which seems complicated at the start but has a simple explanation. Consider the following position. In this position it is Black to play, White

65

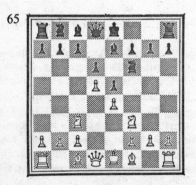

having made five moves to Black's four. If Black plays 5. ...,
P–B4; then White can reply, if he likes, with 6. P × P *en passant*
(French for 'in passing') and we would get the position as in
Diagram 66.

66

At first glance the whole transaction may appear mysterious
and almost a conjuring trick. But it has a solid and logical basis
in the history of the game. When chess was first invented, round
about the fifth century A.D. in North-West India (according to
most authorities), pawns could move only one square at a time.
But after the game came to Europe in the early Middle Ages the
practice gradually arose of moving the pawn two squares at a
time on its first move and if it was so desired. To compensate for
this the *en passant* rule was instituted, by which one could capture
a pawn if it moved two squares, just as if it had moved only one
square, always providing one had a pawn on the fifth rank. I
use the words 'could' and 'if one likes' for the reason that
one does not have to take the pawn *en passant* but can leave it
standing on its fourth rank.

The same opportunities for taking *en passant* are open to Black.
If he has a pawn on his fifth rank and White plays a pawn past
it from White's second rank to White's fourth rank, then Black
can capture it *en passant*. Look at the position in Diagram 67.

Here both sides have made five moves and now, if White plays 6. P–KN4, Black can, if he so wishes, reply 6. ..., P × P e.p. (the abbreviated version of *en passant* which is employed in writing a game score) and we get the position in Diagram 68.

## THE ALGEBRAIC NOTATION

In Chapter 2 I described the descriptive notation which is used in English- and Spanish-speaking countries. But there is another notation, the algebraic, which is employed in the rest of the world and which is even gaining ground over the descriptive both here and in America. At the moment, the majority of players in Britain use the descriptive notation, but I would not be surprised if, in a few years' time, the descriptive were to be superseded by the algebraic here too. For reasons that will become clear soon enough, the algebraic enjoys certain advantages over the descriptive.

In the algebraic notation the eight files, looking at the board from left to right for White, are lettered from a to h. Thus the QR file is lettered a, the QN file is b, and so on to the KR file which is h. Each rank is numbered from 1 to 8.

This means that each square is represented by a letter and a number. Thus QR1 (in the descriptive) becomes a1, QR2 is a2, QR3 is a3 and so on. The whole board is lettered and numbered as in Diagram 69.

69

| a8 | b8 | c8 | d8 | e8 | f8 | g8 | h8 |
|----|----|----|----|----|----|----|----|
| a7 | b7 | c7 | d7 | e7 | f7 | g7 | h7 |
| a6 | b6 | c6 | d6 | e6 | f6 | g6 | h6 |
| a5 | b5 | c5 | d5 | e5 | f5 | g5 | h5 |
| a4 | b4 | c4 | d4 | e4 | f4 | g4 | h4 |
| a3 | b3 | c3 | d3 | e3 | f3 | g3 | h3 |
| a2 | b2 | c2 | d2 | e2 | f2 | g2 | h2 |
| a1 | b1 | c1 | d1. | e1 | f1 | g1 | h1 |

The advantage of this system is that each square has the same name for both White and Black. White's QR1 is a1 for both sides and Black's QR1 is a8 for both sides. This already represents a great saving in space and time.

The pieces, with the exception of the pawns, are represented by their initial letters, just as in the descriptive. But when a pawn moves, no special indication as to the nature of the piece is necessary. For the complete move you add the name of the square to which you move your piece. Thus N–KB3 becomes, for White, Nf3; and if Black plays N–KB3, that becomes Nf6. This is short enough, but even shorter is the representation of a pawn move. *1*. P–K4, P–K4 becomes, in algebraic, *1*. e4, e5; and *1*. P–K4, P–K3; *2*. P–Q4, P–Q4; *3*. P–K5, becomes *1*. e4, e6; *2*. d4, d5; *3*. e5.

When two similar pieces can go to the same square you indicate which one it is by adding, to the initial letter of the piece, the letter of the square the piece has left. Thus, in Diagram 70, if it

70

is White's move and he wishes to play KR–R3 this is, in algebraic, Rha3; if he wants to play the QR to R3, then that is Raa3. If he wants to play N(K2)–B3, then that is Nec3; if he wants to move the other Knight there, then it is Ndc3. If it is Black's turn to move and he wants to move KN–B3, then that is Ngf6; if he wants to move the other Knight there, then that is Ndf6.

The symbols for castling are the same as in the descriptive notation: O–O for King-side castling and O–O–O for Queen-side castling. Captures can be indicated either by × as in descriptive or by the addition of : and the latter practice seems to be gaining the upper hand nowadays. Thus N × B in the position in Diagram 70 is Ne7: (or N×e7). Pawn captures do not even need the capture symbol. Thus, if Black plays (in Diagram 70) g6 and White wishes to capture the pawn in reply, then that is simply hg. The symbol for capturing *en passant*, which is e.p. in the descriptive, is superfluous in the algebraic, though it is permissible in such cases to add the number to the letter of the square on which one captures. Thus if, in Diagram 70, Black plays g5 (which is P–KN4 in descriptive) White may capture *en passant* by hg6.

There is a longer form of the algebraic which consists in giving the square of departure as well as the square of arrival. In this P–K4, which is simply e4 in algebraic, becomes, in the longer form, e2–e4. But this is old-fashioned and rarely used since it abandons one of the advantages of the algebraic in taking up as much time and space as the descriptive.

As an illustration of a whole game in algebraic, I give a recent brevity from the British Championship at Chester, 1979, indicating the descriptive equivalent in brackets after the move.

| WHITE: J. HALL | BLACK: W. WATSON |
|---|---|
| *1.* e4 (P–K4) | c5 (P–QB4) |
| *2.* Nf3 (N–KB3) | d6 (P–Q3) |
| *3.* d4 (P–Q4) | cd (P × P) |
| *4.* Nd4: (N × P) | Nf6 (N–KB3) |
| *5.* Nc3 (N–QB3) | g6 (P–KN3) |
| *6.* Be3 (B–K3) | Bg7 (B–N2) |
| *7.* f3 (P–B3) | Nc6 (N–B3) |
| *8.* Qd2 (Q–Q2) | O–O (O–O) |
| *9.* O–O–O (O–O–O) | Nd4: (N × N) |
| *10.* Bd4: (B × N) | Be6 (B–K3) |
| *11.* Nd5 (N–Q5) | Bd5: (B × N) |
| *12.* ed5: (P × B) | Qc7 (Q–B2) |
| *13.* h4 (P–KR4) | Rfc8 (KR–B1) |
| *14.* h5 (P–R5) | Bh6 (B–R3) |

White resigns, since if he plays *15.* Qh6: then Black mates by *15.* . . ., Qc2:. Or if *15.* Be3, Be3: *16.* Qe3: Qc2: mate.

71

Final position

I do not wish to prejudice you against one or other of the notations, since it is in the last instance just a matter of what one gets used to. Neither notation is inherently difficult or at any stage difficult to grasp. But I would point out that as a matter of economy it pays to use the algebraic which can save one using quite a lot of symbols, as you can see from the game I have given.

EXERCISES

72

1. Can White now play *1*. P–N8 = Q ch, in view of the fact that he already has a Queen?

73

**2.** White to play – should he play *1*. P–B8 = Q?

74

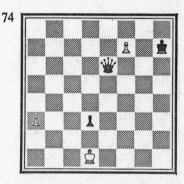

**3.** White to play – what move should he play?

75

4. If White now plays P–QN4 what move, if any, can Black play with his QBP?

76

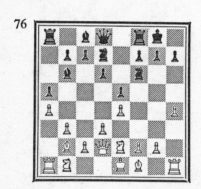

5. If you count the moves each side has made in this position, you will discover they have each made eight and that it is White's turn to move. He is hesitating between playing 9. QN–B3 and 9. R–KR3. How would you express these moves in algebraic notation?

**6.** Play out the following game which occurred in the 1979 British Championship at Chester.

WHITE: P. LITTLEWOOD      BLACK: J. PENROSE

*1.* d4, d5; *2.* c4, dc; *3.* Nf3, a6; *4.* e3, Nf6; *5.* Bc4:, e6; *6.* O–O, c5; *7.* a4, Nc6; *8.* Qe2, Qc7; *9.* Nc3, Bd6; *10.* Kh1, O–O; *11.* dc, Bc5:; *12.* e4, Ng4; *13.* Ba2, Nd4; and White resigns. He cannot play *14.* Nd4:, because of *14.* …, Qh2: mate. Whilst if he plays *14.* Qd1, he is mated after *14.* …, Nf3:; *15.* Qf3:, Qh2: etc.

## ANSWERS TO THE EXERCISES

**1.** (see Diagram 72) Yes, he can play *1.* P–N8 = Q ch. The fact that he already has a Queen does not affect the issue. He can make as many Queens as he likes.

**2.** (see Diagram 73) No, he should not play *1.* P–B8 = Q since then Black gets a draw by stalemate. Correct would be *1.* P–B8 = R since then he can very easily force mate.

**3.** (see Diagram 74) White should not play *1.* P–B8 = Q, because then he is mated after *1.* …, Q–K7 ch; *2.* K–B1, Q–B7. But he should play *1.* P–B8 = N ch, K–N2; *2.* N × Q ch, with an easy win.

**4.** (see Diagram 75) If White plays *1.* P–QN4, Black can reply *1.* …, P × P e.p. when he removes the White QNP and places his own pawn on QN6.

**5.** (see Diagram 76) *9.* QN–B3 is, in algebraic, *9.* Nbc3. And *9.* R–KR3 is in algebraic *9.* Rh3.

6. The game plays out as follows: *1.* d4 (P–Q4), d5 (P–Q4); *2.* c4 (P–QB4), dc (P × P); *3.* Nf3 (N–KB3), a6 (P–QR3); *4.* e3 (P–K3), Nf6 (N–KB3); *5.* Bc4: (B × P), e6 (P–K3); *6.* O–O, c5 (P–B4);

77

7. a4 (P–QR4), Nc6 (N–B3); *8.* Qe2 (Q–K2), Qc7 (Q–B2); *9.* Nc3 (N–B3), Bd6 (B–Q3); *10.* Kh1 (K–R1), O–O; *11.* dc (P × P), Bc5: (B × P); *12.* e4 (P–K4), Ng4 (N–KN5); *13.* Ba2 (B–R2), Nd4 (N–Q5); and White resigns.

78

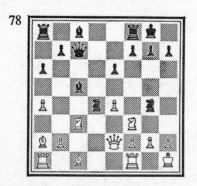

Final position

72

# CHAPTER 5

# MORE DIFFICULT TYPES OF MATE

The types of mate I am now going to describe are indeed more difficult than checkmate with the two Rooks or with the Queen, but they are, nevertheless, quite common. In fact, the more you play the more you will meet these more difficult types and, once you master the ideas behind the mating processes, you will have learnt a great deal about the game and will be in a position to understand quite a lot that a good and competent player knows.

In these endings, as in all endings, the utmost use must be made of the King. The reason for this is that, unlike those occasions when you have (for example) two Rooks, you cannot deliver mate with the piece alone. So you will soon see that the King has a peculiar attacking power of its own. Since it cannot be placed on the square adjacent to the enemy King, it follows that the enemy too must keep his distance and so, by approaching the opposing King with your own, you can force it back.

In all these mating endings the basic principle is the same – restriction of space to the enemy – as we saw in Chapter 2 when looking at the simpler mates. So, bearing this in mind, let us look at the commonest type of mate.

### MATE WITH KING AND ROOK AGAINST KING

Here, just as in the mate with King and Queen, the two pieces work hand-in-hand and the co-operation between King and Rook is, if possible, even closer. The King forms a sort of cordon or net round the enemy King in conjunction with the Rook. In order to restrict the amount of space the enemy King has, you have to tighten this net continually, always bearing in mind the necessity of not allowing the opposing King to escape from the net.

The end-objective, then, is to drive the King back to the edge or side of the board, where it has less chance of escaping from the net, and then to force it into a corner where mate can be delivered. Diagram 79 shows one of the final positions at which you should aim. White plays and gives checkmate by R−B8.

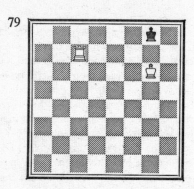

79

How does one arrive at this final position? Consider what the position was like one move earlier for both sides. In all probability the Black King was on R1 since, if it had been on B1, it would have tried to escape from the net by going to K1. And the White King might well have been on B6, as in Diagram 80. In this

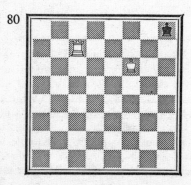

80

position White closes up the net tightly by playing K – N6. Black is forced to reply K – N1 and White mates by R – B8.

This sort of checkmate can be achieved in any corner of the board. And if the opponent is careless and comes quietly, then of course he can be mated away from the corner, though always on the edge of the board. Look at the position in Diagram 81

81

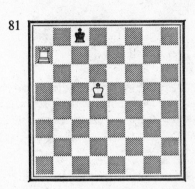

for an example of how mate can be delivered in another corner of the board and how the opponent can make it easy for you if so inclined.

White is to play and has already won more than half the battle in that he has the enemy King confined to the edge or back rank. He plays *1*. K – Q6, and if now Black is so incautious as to play *1*. ..., K – Q1; then he is mated by *2*. R – R8.

Therefore Black replies *1*. ..., K – N1; attacking the Rook. White plays *2*. R – QB7, which leaves Black with only *2*. ..., K – R1; and, now that we have done all that we can do with the Rook we use the King with *3*. K – B6, K – N1; and still using the King, *4*. K – N6, K – R1; *5*. R – B8 mate.

So far, we have been looking at finishes in which the enemy King is already on the edge of the board. How, if the King is in the centre, is it to be induced to go to the edge?

82

In this position, as in many similar positions, the power of the King as an attacking force is particularly striking, as White's opening move shows:

| | |
|---|---|
| 1. K–B6 | K–Q5 |
| 2. R–K1 | |

The idea is to force the King to a back rank, in this case the QR file. Had the opposing King gone back, say with 1. ..., K–K4; we would have started to force it back to an edge on the other side of the board by 2. R–R4.

| | |
|---|---|
| 2. ... | K–B5 |

(Or he could play 2. ..., K–Q6 with much the same result, as we would then play 3. K–Q5, K–Q7; 4. R–K4.) But after Black's K–B5 we can force him nearer the edge by the direct

| | |
|---|---|
| 3. R–K4 ch | K–Q6 |
| 4. K–Q5 | |

And the Black King must go nearer the corner with

| | |
|---|---|
| 4. ... | K–B6 |

Now we cut off the King from the Q file by

| | |
|---|---|
| 5. R–Q4 | K–B7 |

If the King had gone to either N6 or N7, then the Rook would have cut him off from the B file by 6. R–QB4.

So now it is the King's turn to be useful with

      6. K–B4                           K–N7

(Or Black may play 6. K–B8; when 7. K–B3, would effectively cut off Black's escape from the edge.)

Once again the Rook can check back the King with

      7. R–Q2 ch                     K–B8
      8. K–B3

And, if you look back at the position in Diagram 81, you will see we have a similar set-up on the other edge of the board.

You use the same type of play: 8. ..., K–N8; 9. K–N3, K–B8; and the Rook moves back along the Q file, anywhere, say 10. R–Q8, K–N8; 11. R–Q1 mate. Observe how the Rook wastes a move or, rather, makes a waiting move so as to induce the enemy King into a mating position.

What also becomes very clear when you consider the examples of mating technique already given is the way the mating process is a joint operation in which, curiously enough, the senior partner is the piece which has the lesser range. It is the invulnerable nature of the King that gives it this special force. Thus, in the following position (Diagram 83) it is best to start off, not by an attempt to cut off the King by R–N4 or R–QB1, but by 1. K–N2.

83

Black's best defence is to try and maintain his King in the centre as long as possible; for, remember, as long as the enemy King is in the centre and you have only one Rook to do the work, you cannot mate it. So he plays *1.* ..., K–Q5; *2.* K–B2, K–K5; and not *2.* ..., K–B5; as you would then cut him off from five-eighths of the board by *3.* R–Q1.

Now, however, you use the Rook to cut him off from the top half of the board by *3.* R–N5. And then comes *3.* ..., K–Q5; *4.* K–N3, K–K5; *5.* K–B3, K–B5; *6.* K–Q3. Note how, just by using the King and avoiding unnecessary checks, you have driven the opposing King right back.

| | |
|---|---|
| *6.* ... | K–N5 |

Only if now he had played *6.* ..., K–B6; would you have checked him back by *7.* R–B5 ch.

| | |
|---|---|
| *7.* K–K3 | K–N6. |

Forced, if *7.* ..., K–R5; *8.* K–B3, K–R6; *9.* R–R5 mate. But now, with the Kings opposite each other, you do use the Rook to check him back.

| | |
|---|---|
| *8.* R–N5 ch | K–R5 |
| *9.* K–B4 | K–R6 |
| *10.* K–B3 | K–R7 |

If the Black King attacks the Rook by *10.* ..., K–R5; then you move back anywhere along the rank, say *11.* R–K5, and after *11.* ..., K–R6; mate him by *12.* R–R5 mate.

But now perhaps one might think of checking the King? Yes, but not by *11.* R–N2 ch, K–R8; *12.* K–N3, when you have merely succeeded in stalemating the opponent.

No, correct is *11.* R–R5 ch, K–N8; and now you waste your move with the Rook by, say, *12.* R–R6, K–B8; *13.* R–R1 mate.

As a matter of fact, a couple of moves ago there was another way of administering mate in exactly the same number of moves. Leaving the White King on B3, put the Rook back to KN5 and the Black King back to R7. Then you can also mate by *11.* R–N7 (or to N6 or N8) and Black must reply *11.* ..., K–R8 since *11.* ..., K–R6 allows mate by *12.* R–R7.

With the enemy King right in the corner, you use your King to close the net with *12*. K–B2, K–R7; *13*. R–R7 mate.

So, to sum up, the mating process can be divided into three parts:

1. Using the King and Rook in close collaboration, you drive the enemy King to the back rank.

2. The enemy King is forced into a corner.

3. By the use of a waiting move with the Rook you force the King into a mating net.

Always have it in mind to make the utmost use of your King as the attacker and, as the defender, try to maintain your King in the centre. Avoid stalemates along the lines already indicated and don't leave your Rook to be taken by the enemy King through a fit of absent-mindedness!

There is so much of chess in this King and Rook mate that it is worthwhile studying and restudying each of the positions I have given. Also, try yourself out by putting up positions with King and Rook against King, other than the ones given in this book. Then do your best to work them out, using the examples I have given as your guides. To assist you in this, here are some exercises given in increasing order of difficulty. You will find the solutions at the end of this chapter.

### EXERCISES

84

1. White to play and mate in one.

85

**2.** White to play and mate in two.

86

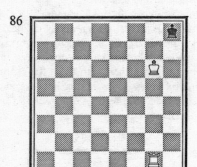

**3.** White to play and mate in two.

87

4. White to play and mate in three.

88

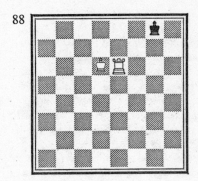

5. White to mate in five.

89

**6.** White to mate in twelve.


### MATE WITH KING AND TWO BISHOPS AGAINST KING

This is rather less common than the mate with the Rook and, to my mind, a little more difficult. When one realizes that two Bishops constitute a stronger force than the Rook, it is a little surprising that the process should appear more difficult. Perhaps it is because one has less practice with it; but it remains a fact that as a rule it takes longer to mate with the Bishops than with the Rook (for more about the comparative value of the pieces see Chapter 8, page 169).

The actual process is easy enough to understand. You bring the two Bishops to work together and again, just as in the mate with the Rook, take care to make use of your King in order to narrow down on the enemy.

It is essential to drive the enemy King into a corner; for Bishops work on diagonals only and do not have the lateral or vertical power of the Rook. Once you have got the King into a corner, you establish your own King a Knight's move away from the enemy (i.e. on N6 or B7) and can then deliver mate as in Diagram 90. Here White gives mate by B–Q4.

90

The longest it should take to mate with the Bishops is, from the worst position, eighteen moves. The worst position is one where the two Bishops and the King are far apart and you have to spend some time to make them work in unison, as in Diagram 91. Note that the Black King is about as far away as possible

91

from a corner and, if he wants to avoid being mated, he must try and keep the King in the centre as much as possible.

The first task for White is to get his pieces working together whilst at the same time cutting the Black King off from escape to other parts of the board. So he plays:

*1.* B–KN6                    K–Q4

Black keeps in the centre as far as possible.

|                | |                |
| -------------- |-| -------------- |
| 2. B–N6        | | K–B3           |

If he had played 2. ..., K–K4; White would still have replied 3. B–K3.

|                | |                |
| -------------- |-| -------------- |
| 3. B–K3        | | K–Q4           |
| 4. B–Q3        | |                |

Now that the two Bishops are together, note how much more powerful they have become and how they limit Black's moves. White's next task is to bring his King into action and to join it up with the combination of forces formed by the two Bishops.

|                | |                |
| -------------- |-| -------------- |
| 4. ...         | | K–K4           |
| 5. K–B7        | |                |

A semi-waiting move that in fact forces the enemy King to give ground.

|                | |                |
| -------------- |-| -------------- |
| 5. ...         | | K–Q4           |
| 6. K–B6        | | K–Q3           |
| 7. B–K4        | | K–Q2           |

After 7. ..., K–B2; 8. K–K7, forces the enemy King to the back rank and, by making it go near the corner, shortens the mating process.

|                |
| -------------- |
| 8. B–B4        |

Now the Black King has to go to the back rank and White takes steps to force it to the corner nearer his own King. Without the co-operation of the White King the Bishops cannot mate by themselves.

|                | |                |
| -------------- |-| -------------- |
| 8. ...         | | K–B1           |
| 9. K–K6        | | K–Q1           |
| 10. B–N7       | | K–K1           |
| 11. B–B7       | | K–B1           |
| 12. K–B6       | |                |

Not *12*. B–B6, when the Black King escapes from the corner by *12*. ..., K–N2.

|      |        |        |
|------|--------|--------|
| *12*. ... | K–K1 |
| *13*. B–B6 ch | K–B1 |
| *14*. B–Q6 ch | K–N1 |

Now comes one of the most important moves in the whole sequence of forcing the King into the corner. As I said when describing the mating process at the beginning of the section, the King is to be placed a Knight's move away from the enemy.

|      |        |        |
|------|--------|--------|
| *15*. K–N6! | K–R1 |

Now, how does White continue? If you look at the position you will see that if it were Black's turn to move he would have to play *16*. ..., K–N1; when White could mate him in two moves by *17*. B–Q5 ch, K–R1; *18*. B–K5 mate. So what White must now do is to waste a move whilst maintaining the net round the enemy King. This means he has to find a waiting move that threatens nothing but does not create a loophole for Black's King to escape. He must not, for example, play *16*. B–Q5, since that would be stalemate. But there are quite a number of moves that will fill the bill here.

|      |        |        |
|------|--------|--------|
| *16*. B–K7 (or B–B5 | |
|     or B–N4 or B–R3) | K–N1 |
| *17*. B–Q5 ch | K–R1 |
| *18*. B–B6 mate. | |

If you go back to the position on White's sixteenth move, when the Bishops were on Q6 and QB6 and the White King was on N6, you will find that White could also have mated by *16*. K–R6, K–N1; *17*. B–Q5 ch, K–R1; *18*. B–K5 mate.

92

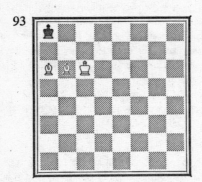

7.  White to play and mate in three moves.

93

8.  White to play and mate in four moves.

94

9. White to play and mate in eight moves.

95

10. White to play and mate in ten moves.

Perhaps I should say here that if you find these exercises too difficult to work out at this early stage in your development as a player, no great harm will be done if you look at the answers if you fail to find the solutions. For the main point of these exercises is to show you how various positions involving this type of mate can be treated properly and with the least waste of time and energy.

### ANSWERS TO THE EXERCISES

1. (see Diagram 84) White mates by *1*. R–R8.

2. (see Diagram 85) White mates by *1*. R–K5, K–B1; *2*. R–K8.

3. (see Diagram 86) White mates by *1.* K-B7, K-R2; *2.* R-KR1. Note that a dreadful mistake would be *1.* K-R6, when stalemate occurs.

4. (see Diagram 87) White mates in three by *1.* R-QR5, and if *1.* ..., K-K1; *2.* R-Q5, K-B1; *3.* R-Q8. Or if *1.* ..., K-N1; *2.* R-R5, K-B1; *3.* R-R8 mate.

5. (see Diagram 88) White mates in five by *1.* K-K7, K-N2; *2.* R-C6, K-N1; *3.* K-B6, and now Black can choose between *3.* ..., K-R2; *4.* K-B7, K-R1; *5.* R-KR6 and *3.* ..., K-R1; *4.* K-N6, K-N1; *5.* R-Q8.

6. see (Diagram 89) White mates in twelve by *1.* R-K1 ch, K-B4; *2.* K-Q4, K-B5; *3.* R-B1 ch, K-N4; *4.* K-K4, K-N3; *5.* K-K5, K-N4; *6.* R-N1 ch, K-R5; and White now has two ways of mating, each of which takes six more moves:

(A) *7.* K-E5, K-R6; *8.* K-B4, K-R7; *9.* R-N3, K-R8; *10.* K-B3, K-R7; *11.* K-B2, K-R8; *12.* R-R3 mate.

(B) *7.* K-B4, K-R6; *8.* R-N3 ch, K-R7 (after *8.* ..., K-R5; White mates by *9.* R-K3, K-R4; *10.* R-K6, K-R5; *11.* R-KR6); *9.* K-B3, K-R8; *10.* K-B2, K-R7; *11.* R-B3, K-R8; *12.* R-KR3.

7. (see Diagram 92) White mates by *1.* B-K3 ch, K-R2; *2.* B-E5 ch, K-R1; *3.* B-Q4 mate.

8. (see Diagram 93) White mates by *1.* B-E5, K-N1; *2.* K-N6, K-R1; *3.* B-N7 ch, K-N1; *4.* B-Q6 mate. The Bishop could in fact have gone back on the first move to anywhere along the diagonal QE5-KN1 so as to give mate eventually on the diagonal Q6-KR2.

9. (see Diagram 94) White mates by *1.* B-Q4, K-N4; *2.* B-QB5, K-R4; *3.* K-B6, K-R3; *4.* B-N4, K-R2; *5.* K-B7, K-R3; *6.* B-Q3 ch, K-R2; *7.* B-B5 ch, K-R1; *8.* B-K4 mate.

10. (see Diagram 95) White mates by *1.* K-B5, K-Q2; *2.* B-B5, K-B2; *3.* K-K6, K-Q1; *4.* B-N6 ch, K-K1; *5.* B-B6 ch, K-B1; *6.* K-E6, K-N1; *7.* K-N6, K-B1; *8.* B-B5 ch, K-N1; *9.* B-Q5 ch, K-R1; *10.* B-Q4 mate.

# CHAPTER 6

# HOW TO OPEN WITH WHITE

At the beginning of the game all the pieces are stationed on the back rank where they are inactive and, as it were, asleep. If you have the White pieces then you have the move, and your primary objective should be to bring out your pieces in such a way that they can work together to attack and conquer the enemy.

In short, you have to *develop* your pieces. No player, however good – or however bad, for that matter – can play chess without developing his pieces; this is a basic requirement, whether you are world champion or absolute beginner.

So the aim is simple enough; but there is one consideration that complicates the issue; unless it is understood and its requirements carried out, you have no chance of becoming a good or a competent player. The pieces must be so developed that they can co-operate and form a massive power of attack against Black. This means that it is no use developing in a haphazard manner; the opening must be planned as carefully as a general plans the opening stages of a battle campaign. Remember that chess was in origin a war-game: wars are won by those who form the better plans, and lost by those whose plans are faulty or non-existent.

The question now arises – how are the pieces to be developed. If you look at the initial position you will find that, apart from the pawns, the only pieces that can move are the Knights, since the pawns themselves shut in the other pieces: the Rooks, the Bishops and the Queen and King.

If you confine yourself to moving the pawns and the Knights and then try and attack the enemy at once with this combined force you will be repulsed with heavy losses by an enemy who has developed all his pieces. So what is wanted is a few pawn moves, a few Knight moves and then attention can and must be paid to developing the other pieces.

As a general rule those openings that demand the fewest pawn moves are the best; you will find that the openings I am now going to describe fit in with this requirement. The four I have chosen – the Giuoco Piano, the King's Gambit, the Ruy Lopez and the Queen's Gambit – are all both ancient and modern in that time has shown that they are the soundest and best means of attack. None of them is particularly difficult to understand and yet, once you do understand them and have worked out how to use them to develop your forces properly, you will have made considerable progress towards becoming a good chess-player.

For your first move you need a pawn move that will allow you to develop as many pieces as possible and this gives us the first move for either side:

### *1.* P–K4

With this move lines of action are opened up for both the KB and the Queen. But the double advance of the pawn does more than that. A single advance of the pawn would also achieve the dual development of Bishop and Queen. But look at the board and you will discover that it is in fact divided into two halves, the first four ranks belonging to White and the other four ranks to Black.

This means that by playing *1.* P–K4, White attacks two squares in the enemy camp, Black's Q4 and KB4 and, since it is always desirable to combine development with aggression, the double advance of the pawn is that much superior to the single step.

### *1.* ...                    P–K4

Exactly the same considerations apply to Black's first move as to White's. However, he can play other moves as we shall see in the next chapter, which looks at the game from the Black point of view.

### *2.* N–KB3

A good developing move which at the same time attacks the enemy pawn. White could achieve the same purpose with *2.* Q–R5, but this would be a bad move since eventually the

Queen would have to retire with loss of time. For what would happen then would be, for example, *2.* ..., N–QB3; and if *3.* N–KB3, again attacking the enemy pawn, then *3.* ..., N–B3 attacking the Queen, when *4.* Q–B5, P–Q3; *5.* Q–N5, P–KR3; beats back the Queen with gain of time and position for Black.

| *2.* ... | N–QB3 |
|---|---|

Black defends his pawn and develops his own Knight.

Now comes the move for White which characterizes the

### GIUOCO PIANO

96

*3.* B–B4

This developing move which characterizes the Giuoco Piano (the Quiet Game, so called by the Italians with whom it was already popular some three centuries ago) has a lot to be said for it. Placed as it is on a diagonal running from QB4 to KB7, the Bishop bears down on Black's KB2 which is the weakest point in the vicinity of the Black King, this being the only square that is not defended at least twice. At the same time it prepares the way for White to castle, which would automatically bring the KR into some play at any rate.

Black now imitates White, since otherwise he is going to lose ground in the development of his King-side pieces.

| *3.* ... | B–B4 |
|---|---|

In this position, White can continue with his development in any one of three ways: 4. O–O, or 4. N–B3, or 4. P–Q3. Experience has shown that in every case, by continuing with his own development (i.e. by imitating White), Black can gain equality in position. For example: 4. O–O, N–B3; 5. P–Q3, P–Q3; or 4. N–B3, N–B3; 5. P–Q3, P–Q3; 6. B–KN5, N–QR4; and in both cases Black stands well.

Hence White must evolve another idea which, whilst not neglecting development, concentrates on improving his position in the centre. This he does with

4. P–B3

The idea of this move is to follow it up with 5. P–Q4, and then, after Black has exchanged pawns, to retake with the pawn, thereby creating an imposing-looking centre.

Why this concentration on the centre? There are a number of reasons but two of them are fairly obvious and convincing. In the first place, you can see that if White establishes his pawns on Q4 and K4 he will greatly impede and interfere with the development of the Black pieces. The second idea is really one which arises out of the first, but it is far more important and is a basic idea behind all openings. The fact that the centre pawns interfere with the development of the enemy pieces shows that a command, or at any rate the use, of the centre is vital for the further and continuous development of the pieces. You can best see what I mean by imagining that you have a square-shaped city in which all the roads lead to and through the centre. If for any reason there is a blockage in the centre that prevents you from travelling through it, then you cannot get from one part of the city to the other. So it is with the chess-board and its centre.

To return to the Giuoco Piano: Black continues with his development and attacks White's KP with

4. ...                              N–B3

And White proceeds with his plan of building up the centre.

5. P–Q4                          P × P
6. P × P                          B–N5 ch

Black must react as vigorously as possible, since if he retreats with the Bishop by 6. ..., B–N3; White chases the QN away with 7. P–Q5.

> 7. B–Q2

The soundest line; after 7. N–B3, N×KP; 8. O–O, B×N; Black has at least equality.

> 7. ...                           B×B ch

This too is the prudent course. Black has to submit to a strong attack after 7. ..., N×KP; 8. B×B, N×B; 9. B×P ch, K×B; 10. Q–N3 ch, P–Q4; 11. N–K5 ch, K–K3; 12. Q×N, P–B4; 13. Q–R3.

> 8. QN×B                          P–Q4
> 9. P×P                           KN×P
> 10. Q–N3

Increasing the pressure on Black's Q4 and, indirectly, on his KB2 square.

> 10. ...                          N(B3)–K2

Black in turn tries to increase his hold on the vital Q4 square.

> 11. O–O                          O–O
> 12. KR–K1

12. N–K5, with its attack on Black's KB2, also holds out possibilities; but it is better to get another piece into action.

> 12. ...                          P–QB3

We have now really reached the middle game and left the opening stages. White has an advantage in space, in particular on the K file where his Rook is powerfully placed and where he can post his Knight in an admirable attacking position on K5.

Looking for a game played by a great master to demonstrate the possibilities of the Giuoco Piano, I thought I would go back in time to the middle of the last century and give a game won by that greatest of all masters in the open positions, Paul Morphy. This game was played in Paris in 1863.

WHITE: PAUL MORPHY      BLACK: A. DE RIVIÈRE

| | | |
|---|---|---|
| 1. | P–K4 | P–K4 |
| 2. | N–KB3 | N–QB3 |
| 3. | B–B4 | B–B4 |
| 4. | P–B3 | Q–K2 |

As will soon be seen, the Queen is not well placed here. Better is 4. ..., N–B3.

| | | |
|---|---|---|
| 5. | P–Q4 | B–N3 |
| 6. | O–O | P–Q3 |
| 7. | P–KR3 | N–B3 |
| 8. | R–K1 | P–KR3 |
| 9. | P–QR4 | P–QR4 |
| 10. | N–R3 | N–Q1 |

Waste of time; the intention is to play P–B3 if White plays N–QN5, but White plans quite another future for the Knight and better therefore was 10. ..., O–O.

| | | |
|---|---|---|
| 11. | N–B2 | B–K3 |
| 12. | N–K3 | B × B |
| 13. | N × B | N–Q2 |
| 14. | N–K3! | P–N3 |

To prevent N–B5; but he has now created a serious weakness on the King's wing.

|  |  |  |
|---|---|---|
| *15.* N–Q5 | | Q–K3 |

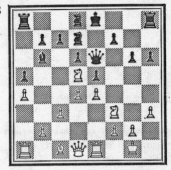

98

|  |  |  |
|---|---|---|
| *16.* B × P | | P–KB3 |

After 16. ..., R × B; *17.* N–N5 wins the Queen.

|  |  |  |
|---|---|---|
| *17.* B–N7 | | R–R4 |
| *18.* P–KN4 | | R × P |
| *19.* N × KBP ch | | N × N |
| *20.* N–N5 | | Q–Q2 |

Hoping for *21.* N × R, when Q × B would give him a reasonable game; but White does not oblige, and better would have been *20.* ..., Q–K2.

|  |  |  |
|---|---|---|
| *21.* B × N | | R–R5 |
| *22.* P–B3 | | P × P |
| *23.* P × P | | R–KR3 |
| *24.* K–N2 | | N–B2 |
| *25.* R–R1 | | N × N |

Or *25.* ..., R × R; *26.* Q × R, N × N; *27.* Q–R8 ch, K–B2; *28.* Q–N7 ch, when Black can choose between *28.* ..., K–K3; *29.* P–Q5 mate and *28.* ..., K–K1; *29.* Q–N8 mate.

|  |  |  |
|---|---|---|
| *26.* R × R | | N–R2 |
| *27.* Q–R1 | | N × B |

| 28. R–R8 ch | K–K2 |
| 29. R × R | B × P |
| 30. Q–R6 | Q–B3 |
| 31. R–QB1 | Q–N3 |
| 32. R × P ch! | K–K3 |

If *32.* ..., Q × R; *33.* Q–N7 ch, picking up the Queen.

| 33. R–K8 ch | N × R |
| 34. Q × P ch | K–K4 |
| 35. Q–B5 mate. | |

## THE KING'S GAMBIT

In direct contrast to the Giuoco Piano, the Quiet Opening, is the violent and far from peaceful King's Gambit which sacrifices material, sometimes as much as a piece (Knight or Bishop) in an all-out attempt to break through Black's defences. The word Gambit is employed for the sacrifice of material, usually a pawn and usually in the opening, in order to gain some compensatory advantage in position.

The sacrifice in the King's Gambit has as its primary objective the opening up of the KB file in order to strike at Black's weakest point, his KB2 square. This is a subsidiary aim, and it is this that in fact gives the King's Gambit its positional meaning and, in so far as this highly disputed field allows, its positional validity or, as perhaps it would be better put, its practical value and its controversial but, nevertheless, undoubted importance from the point of view of opening theory.

The opening was highly popular in the nineteenth century but lost its popularity in our century once it was realized how drawish violent openings tend to become. This is a paradox which I hope to make clear as my description of the lines of this opening proceeds.

The King's Gambit Accepted divides up into two main lines: the King's Knight's Gambit (*1.* P–K4, P–K4; *2.* P–KB4, P × P; *3.* N–KB3) and the King's Bishop's Gambit (*1.* P–K4, P–K4; *2.* P–KB4, P × P; *3.* B–B4). It is with the King's Knight's Gambit that I am concerned, since I regard the King's Bishop's Gambit as unsound. So

*1.* P–K4                                             P–K4

*2.* P–KB4

A frank attempt at opening the KB file which is not without danger for the player who plays the Gambit, since it noticeably opens up his own King's position.

*2.* ...                                             P × P

Black is in fact under no compulsion to accept the Gambit and it is possible that those lines in which he declines the Gambit (to be found later on in this chapter) are superior to the accepted forms for Black.

*3.* N–KB3

The natural move which fends off Q–R5 ch and (very important) brings pressure to bear on the centre.

*3.* ...                                             P–KN4

Again Black can play a kind of delayed Gambit Declined here with such moves as *3.* ..., B–K2; or *3.* ..., N–KB3; or *3.* ..., P–Q4; followed by N–KB3, all of which have their modern supporters (it is in fact these lines that tend to result in draws) and I will defer consideration of these too till I have dealt with the main line (or what I regard as the main line) of the King's Gambit.

*4.* P–KR4

If White is to break through along the KB file then he must undermine the Black diagonal row of pawns in this way.

*4.* ...                                             P–N5

It is clear that *4.* ..., P–KR3 is no protection to the pawn chain since White would then simply play *5.* P × P, and Black could not retake since this would leave his Rook to be captured by the enemy.

*5.* N–K5

The Kieseritsky Gambit, named after a Hungarian grandmaster who made Paris his home more than a hundred years ago and who analysed out this line. It is much superior to the Allgaier Gambit 5. N–N5, which is generally recognized as unsound nowadays. The Kieseritsky has its advantages and its defects. Its chief advantage is that it is concerned with positional problems relating to the control of the centre, and for that reason it has become a favourite with quite a number of modern great players (Bronstein, Spassky and Fischer come readily to mind in this respect). Its disadvantage is that it involves quite a number of moves with the same piece, and this in turn means that White has to be careful not to fall behind in his development.

99

No less than eight lines come into consideration for Black, and I can only give each one space and time enough to afford the reader some glimpse of the possibilities and basic value of each and every line. This should, however, be sufficient to give the beginner some comprehension of the possibilities for both White and Black in the King's Gambit which (like the game of chess itself, for that matter) is surprisingly modern when one considers its ancient origin.

*Line 1*

|       |        |
|-------|--------|
| 5. ...       | N–KB3 |
| 6. P–Q4      |        |

White gambits another pawn in the interests of development and plans to recapture one with his QB, thereby assisting in the main aim of clearing the KB file.

| | |
|---|---|
| 6. ... | P–Q3 |
| 7. N–Q3 | N × P |
| 8. B × P | B–N2 |
| 9. P–B3 | O–O |
| 10. N–Q2 | R–K1 |
| 11. N × N | R × N ch |
| 12. K–B2 | Q–B3 |
| 13. P–KN3 | B–R3 |
| 14. Q–Q2 | N–B3 |
| 15. B–N2 | |

With advantage to White since, despite being a pawn less, he has the better development and will be able to concentrate his Rooks on the vital K and KB files.

*Line 2*

| | |
|---|---|
| 5. ... | N–QB3 |
| 6. P–Q4 | |

This developing central move is often the key move in the Kieseritsky.

| | |
|---|---|
| 6. ... | N × N |
| 7. P × N | P–Q3 |
| 8. B × P | Q–K2 |

An awkwrd-looking move, but still worse would be 8. ..., P × P; 9. Q × Q ch, K × Q; 10. B × P, with considerable advantage to White.

| | |
|---|---|
| 9. P × P | Q × KP ch |
| 10. Q–K2 | Q × Q ch |
| 11. B × Q | B × P |
| 12. B × B | P × B |
| 13. N–B3 | |

With advantage to White as he has a number of weaknesses to hit at in the Black camp.

*Line 3*

| | |
|---|---|
| 5. ... | Q–K2 |

Not a good move, as soon becomes apparent.

| | |
|---|---|
| 6. P–Q4 | P–Q3 |
| 7. N × NP | Q × KP ch |
| 8. Q–K2 | B–B4 |
| 9. B × P | Q × Q ch |
| 10. B × Q | B × P |
| 11. N–B3 | |

And White's great advantage in development gives him much the better game.

*Line 4*

| | |
|---|---|
| 5. ... | B–N2 |

The best line of defence, since it takes advantage of the long diagonal to give the KB much scope for action.

| | |
|---|---|
| 6. P–Q4 | P–Q3 |
| 7. N × NP | B × N |
| 8. Q × B | B × P |
| 9. P–B3 | B–K4 |
| 10. B × P | N–KB3 |
| 11. Q–B3 | QN–Q2 |
| 12. P–KN3 | |

With about a level position.

*Line 5*

| | |
|---|---|
| 5. ... | B–K2 |

Here, despite appearances, the Bishop is not well placed and it is surprising how quickly White can develop an attack on KB7.

| | |
|---|---|
| 6. B–B4 | B × P ch |
| 7. K–B1 | P–Q4 |

|           |          |
|-----------|----------|
| 8. B × P  | N–KR3    |
| 9. P–Q4   | B–N4     |
| 10. N–QB3 |          |

And White is much the better developed.

*Line 6*

|           |          |
|-----------|----------|
| 5. ...    | P–Q3     |
| 6. N × NP | P–KR4    |
| 7. N–B2   | N–KB3    |
| 8. P–Q4   | B–R3     |
| 9. B–K2   |          |

And White's position is better, since his pieces are in better co-operation.

*Line 7*

|           |          |
|-----------|----------|
| 5. ...    | P–Q4     |
| 6. P–Q4   |          |

It is typical of the position that White is able to ignore attacks on his pawns in order to develop as speedily as possible.

|           |          |
|-----------|----------|
| 6. ...    | N–KB3    |
| 7. B × P  | N × P    |
| 8. N–Q2   | N × N    |
| 9. Q × N  |          |

Contrast Black's development with White's and you will see that White has very much the upper hand.

*Line 8*

|           |          |
|-----------|----------|
| 5. ...    | P–KR4    |

An old idea which was surprisingly resuscitated about twenty years ago.

|           |          |
|-----------|----------|
| 6. B–B4   | R–R2     |

This is the point of the line; but it is too defensive in nature.

|           |          |
|-----------|----------|
| 7. P–Q4   | B–R3     |
| 8. N–QB3  | N–QB3    |

100

This position arose in a game Bronstein–Dubinin, 15th U.S.S.R. Championship, 1947, and it continued 9. N × BP, R × N; 10. B × R ch, K × B; 11. B × P, B × B; 12. O–O, Q × P; 13. R × B ch, K–N2; 14. Q–Q2, P–Q3; 15. QR–KB1, N–Q1; 16. N–Q5, B–Q2; 17. P–K5, P × P; 18. P × P, B–B3; 19. P–K6, B × N; 20. R–B7 ch, N × R; 21. R × N ch, K–R1; 22. Q–B3 ch, N–B3; 23. R × N, Q × R; 24. Q × Q ch, K–R2; 25. Q–B5 ch, K–R3; 26. Q × B, K–N3; 27. Q–Q7, resigns.

## REFUSING GAMBITS

You need not accept the pawn offered in a Gambit Opening and, when one is at the learning stage of the game, it is probably safer to reject such offers since, at any rate, not so much book knowledge is required.

There are, basically, two different ways of refusing the Gambit: (1) you do not take the pawn offered but proceed with your development, or (2) you take the pawn but make no attempt to retain it. Both these methods are well illustrated in the lines arising out of the King's Gambit.

*Method 1A*

| | |
|---|---|
| *1.* P–K4 | P–K4 |
| *2.* P–KB4 | P–Q3 |

A passive line which suffers from the disadvantage of shutting in Black's KB. Still worse would be *2. ..., P–KB3; 3. P × P, P × P; 4. Q–R5 ch*, after which Black is in all sorts of trouble.

But Black can play *2. ..., P–Q4* (the Falkbeer Counter-Gambit) which leads to complicated play after *3. KP × P, P–K5; 4. P–Q3, N–KB3; 5. N–Q2, P × P; 6. B × P, N × P.*

|           |        |
|-----------|--------|
| 3. N–KB3  | N–QB3  |
| 4. B–N5   | B–Q2   |
| 5. O–O    | N–B3   |
| 6. P–Q3   | B–K2   |
| 7. N–B3   |        |

Not *7. B × N, B × B; 8. P × P, P × P; 9. N × P*, on account of *9. ..., Q–Q5 ch*, winning the Knight.

|           |        |
|-----------|--------|
| 7. ...    | O–O    |
| 8. K–R1   |        |

Now White is threatening to win the pawn by *9. B × N, B × B; 10. P × P, P × P; 11. N × P.*

|           |        |
|-----------|--------|
| 8. ...    | P × P  |
| 9. B × P  |        |

And White has the advantage.

*Method 1B*

|           |        |
|-----------|--------|
| 1. P–K4   | P–K4   |
| 2. P–KB4  | B–B4   |

A better line than A and one which is based on the sound idea that White has exposed his own King-side to attack by playing P–KB4.

|            |        |
|------------|--------|
| 3. N–KB3   | P–Q3   |
| 4. N–B3    | N–KB3  |
| 5. B–B4    | N–B3   |
| 6. P–Q3    | B–KN5  |
| 7. N–QR4   | B–N3   |
| 8. N × B   | RP × N |

And the position is about level.

*Method 2A*

|       | 1. P–K4      | P–K4  |
|-------|--------------|-------|
|       | 2. P–KB4     | P × P |
|       | 3. N–KB3     | P–Q4  |

Black adopts a policy of freeing his position by counter-attacking in the centre. Such a policy is not without its dangers.

|       | 4. P × P     | N–KB3 |
|-------|--------------|-------|
|       | 5. B–N5 ch   | P–B3  |
|       | 6. P × P     | P × P |
|       | 7. B–B4      | N–Q4  |
|       | 8. N–B3      | B–K2  |
|       | 9. O–O       | O–O   |
|       | 10. P–Q4     | N–N3  |
|       | 11. B–Q3     |       |

And White has a good attacking position.

*Method 2B*

|       | 1. P–K4      | P–K4  |
|-------|--------------|-------|
|       | 2. P–KB4     | P × P |
|       | 3. N–KB3     | B–K2  |

The Cunningham line which gives Black distinct counter-chances.

|       | 4. N–B3      | N–KB3 |

The check with the Bishop is rather deceptive in that, though it disturbs the King, it loses time and space: e.g. *4.* . . ., B–R5 ch; *5.* K–K2, P–Q4; *6.* N × P, N–KB3; *7.* N × N ch, Q × N; *8.* P–Q4, and White commands the centre.

|       | 5. P–K5      | N–N5  |
|-------|--------------|-------|
|       | 6. P–Q4      | N–K6  |
|       | 7. B × N     | P × B |
|       | 8. B–B4      | P–Q3  |
|       | 9. O–O       | O–O   |
|       | 10. Q–Q3     | N–B3  |
|       | 11. P × P    | B × P |

And the position is level.

## THE RUY LOPEZ

The openings we have been looking at so far have been princi-
pally concerned with development, and rightly so. All openings
should be so concerned; but there are other factors to be considered. Chief of these, as I have already made clear, is the control
of the centre. The next two openings, the Ruy Lopez and the
Queen's Gambit, concentrate on this problem.

The Ruy Lopez, so called after a Spanish priest who was Spain's
leading chess-master in the sixteenth century and who wrote a
book in which he analysed the opening, amongst others, has good
claims to be regarded as the most popular of all openings over
the last 300 years. This is a tribute to its strength, but it also means
that it comprises a forest of variations, and here I can only try to
describe the basic idea of the opening and indicate its chief aim.

It starts off with the first two moves of the Giuoco Piano:

| | |
|---|---|
| *1.* P–K4 | P–K4 |
| *2.* N–KB3 | N–QB3 |

Now comes the move that makes it a Ruy Lopez, or a Spanish
Opening, as it is sometimes called.

    *3.* B–N5

A developing move, it is true, but one devoted solely to the
purpose of attacking Black's centre. In fact, the Ruy Lopez could
very well be regarded as an onslaught on Black's K4 square; if
White can induce Black to give up control of that square, then
the first player has won more than half the battle.

Now there are many defences for Black; but the most important and the most popular is the Morphy Defence, named after
the great American master, Paul Morphy, and it is this line I am
going to consider.

| | |
|---|---|
| *3.* ... | P–QR3 |
| *4.* B–R4 | |

Why not *4.* B × N, QP × B; *5.* N × P, winning a pawn? The
answer is, because Black can get the pawn back almost at once
by *5.* ..., Q–Q5.

| | |
|---|---|
| *4.* ... | N–B3 |

It is this counter-attacking move, so characteristic of the vigour of Paul Morphy's style of play, that makes it the Morphy Defence.

### 5. O–O

White does not bother to defend his KP but continues with his developments. As we shall soon see, White can always get his pawn back in any case.

101

Already we have come to a parting of the ways for Black. He can now choose between the Open and the Closed Defence. When we talk about open defences, we mean positions in which the centre is open and in which the pieces, in particular Knights and Bishops, can move to and fro with comparative ease. Closed positions, on the other hand, are the direct opposite. The centre is closed: that is to say, there is an interlocked pawn chain in the centre preventing the easy passage, sometimes any passage, of the minor pieces.

### The Open Defence

     5. ...                   N × P

Black plumps for the Open line, which tends to give him free play for his pieces, but also leaves his pawn position vulnerable to attack.

     6. P–Q4;

Making the centre more open than ever. If now 6. ..., P × P; 7. R–K1, P–Q4; 8. N × P, with advantage to White.

|   |   |
|---|---|
| 6. ... | P–QN4 |
| 7. B–N3 | P–Q4 |

Again, Black would be unwise to take the QP because of 7. ..., P × P; 8. R–K1.

8. P × P

Attacking the QP which Black must now support.

8. ...            B–K3

White must now keep up the pressure on Black's pawn position and not allow Black's pawns to advance on the Queen-side. If he allows Black to play his Queen-side pawns on, then he will lose the initiative.

9. P–B3

A good move that limits the advance of the QP and at the same time plans to deal with the advanced enemy Knight by B–B2 and QN–Q2.

Another line that was popular some twenty years ago is 9. Q–K2, with the plan of attacking the QP by R–Q1.

102

Black, having fallen behind somewhat in the development of his King-side pieces, has now to choose between (1) B–QB4 and (2) B–K2.

(1)

|  |  |
|---|---|
| 9. ... | B–QB4 |
| 10. QN–Q2 | O–O |
| 11. B–B2 |  |

And not *11*. N × N, P × N; *12*. B × B, P × B; when Black has the attack.

|  |  |
|---|---|
| 11. ... | P–B4 |
| 12. N–N3 |  |

Hitting the Bishop and giving White an even stronger grip on the vital Q4 square.

|  |  |
|---|---|
| 12. ... | B–N3 |
| 13. KN–Q4 |  |

And White has a good game with Black having to play very carefully to avoid losing. The game might continue *13.* ..., N × N; *14.* N × N, B × N; *15.* Q × B, P–B4; *16.* Q–Q1, P–B5; *17.* P–B3, with advantage to White.

(2) (see Diagram 102)

|  |  |
|---|---|
| 9. ... | B–K2 |

This move reserves the QB4 square for use by the Knight, or, given the opportunity, for an advance of the QBP.

|  |  |
|---|---|
| 10. QN–Q2 |  |

Partly with the idea of putting pressure on the enemy KN, and partly having in mind an eventual N–QN3 attacking the two vital squares in this variation, Q4 and QB5.

White has a number of alternatives here, the chief of which is *10*. B–K3, when the game could go *10.* ..., O–O; *11*. QN–Q2, N × N; *12*. Q × N, Q–Q2; *13*. Q–Q3, N–R4; *14*. B–B2, P–N3; *15*. B–R6, B–KB4; *16*. Q–K2, KR–K1; with equality (as in a game by correspondence between Keres and Dyckhoff, 1935–6).

As it is, after *10*. QN–Q2, the position is not unlike that reached in the first variation where Black played *9*. ..., B–QB4 and play proceeds for a while in similar fashion.

|  |  |
|---|---|
| 10. ... | O–O |
| 11. B–B2 |  |

Or White may play *11*. Q–K2, to which Black replies *11*. ...,
N–B4 and threatens to exchange Knight for Bishop. In the Ruy
Lopez, White should try and retain this Bishop since it has more
attacking possibilities than any other minor piece. A minor piece
is either a Bishop or a Knight, and major pieces are Queens and
Rooks.

> *11*. ...                 P–B4
> *12*. N–N3

Best; *12*. P × P e.p., N × P (B3) would allow Black attacking
chances on the King-side, since it opens up the file for the KR.

> *12*. ...                 Q–Q2
> *13*. QN–Q4

103

And White has the initiative, though Black also has counter-
attacking chances. The game might continue *13*. ..., N × N;
*14*. N × N, P–B4; *15*. N × B, Q × N; *16*. P–B3, with lines similar
to that in the variation given earlier, where Black plays *9*. ...,
B–QB4.

How dangerous the Open Defence can be for Black was shown
by the following game, the eighth game in the 1979 World
Championship match at Baguio City in the Philippines between
the world champion, Anatoly Karpov, and his challenger,
Viktor Korchnoi.

Karpov had White and the first eight moves went according to the lines shown here: *1.* P–K4, P–K4; *2.* N–KB3, N–QB3; *3.* B–N5, P–QR3; *4.* B–R4, N–B3; *5.* O–O, N × P; *6.* P–Q4, P–QN4; *7.* B–N3, P–Q4; *8.* P × P, B–K3; and now Karpov tried a different move: *9.* QN–Q2, N–B4; *10.* P–B3, P–N3; (a weakening of his King-side for which he has to pay dearly. Correct was *10.* ..., P–Q5).

*11.* Q–K2, B–N2; *12.* N–Q4, N × P; *13.* P–KB4, N–B5; *14.* P–B5, P × P; *15.* N × BP, R–KN1; *16.* N × N, QP × N; *17.* B–B2, N–Q6; *18.* B–R6, B–B1; *19.* QR–Q1, Q–Q4; *20.* B × N, P × B; *21.* R × P, Q–B3; *22.* B × B, Q–N3 ch; *23.* K–R1, K × B; *24.* Q–B3, R–K1; *25.* N–R6, R–N2; *26.* R–Q7, R–QN1 (or *26.* ..., B × R; *27.* Q × P ch, R × Q; *28.* R × R mate).

*27.* N × P, B × R; *28.* N–Q8 dis ch, resigns.

## The Closed Defence

This leads to rather more difficult play (for both sides) than the Open Defence, since both White and Black have to weigh up carefully the respective advantages of purely developing moves and moves that improve the position, in particular from the point of view of control of the centre. However, it is certainly the more popular defence and you will meet it much more often than the Open Line.

Up to Black's fifth move the moves are the same as those in the Open Defence.

|  |  |  |
|---|---|---|
| *1.* P–K4 | | P–K4 |
| *2.* N–KB3 | | N–QB3 |
| *3.* B–N5 | | P–QR3 |
| *4.* B–R4 | | N–B3 |
| *5.* O–O | | B–K2 |

Black tries to keep the centre closed and therefore does not play the Open Defence move *5.* ..., N × P. But now he does threaten to capture the KP on his next move. Hence White protects the pawn and at the same time commences the development of his KR by centralizing it.

<blockquote>6. R–K1        P–QN4</blockquote>

Now that White has protected his KP he threatens B × N followed by N × P; so Black has to weaken his Queen-side a little by advancing his pawns there to chase the Bishop away.

<blockquote>7. B–N3        P–Q3</blockquote>

Preparing to develop his QB and at the same time strengthening his hold on K4.

<blockquote>8. P–B3</blockquote>

He wants to attack Black's centre by P–Q4; but does not like to do so at once because of the line 8. P–Q4, QN × P; 9. N × N, P × N; 10. Q × P?, P–B4; 11. Q moves, P–B5 winning the Bishop.

<blockquote>8. ...        O–O<br>9. P–KR3</blockquote>

Still not P–Q4 because of the danger of the pin (see page 157) on the Knight by the Bishop after 9. P–Q4, B–N5 when White's pawn centre becomes difficult to defend.

<blockquote>9. ...        N–QR4</blockquote>

Hitting the Bishop and preparing an advance of his QBP so as to keep the centre stable.

<blockquote>10. B–B2        P–B4<br>11. P–Q4</blockquote>

Now he strikes hard at Black's K4, and Black has to find a means of holding on to the central point, K4.

<blockquote>11. ...        Q–B2</blockquote>

Suddenly, partly owing to the constant moving of his KB and partly because White has found it necessary to play the preparatory move of P–B3, it becomes apparent that White has been falling behind in development. This applies in particular to the pieces on the Queen's wing. White hastens to rectify all this.

    *12.* QN–Q2

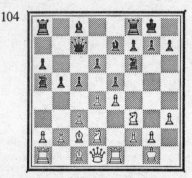

104

Given the time to do so, White will manoeuvre his QN over to the King-side so as to help in the attack there (by N–B1–K3 or N3). How is Black to deal with this dangerous threat? The answer is that there are four main lines, differing in nature in so far as they are dynamic or passive – though perhaps this is putting it a bit too strongly. Rather I should say, the choice is between playing an active, counter-attacking defence and trying to maintain the centre as it is.

*Line 1*

    *12.*   ...                  N–B3

The oldest and still the most popular line. The argument is that this Knight has already performed its duty and that now it should be restored to the centre. There it gives further support to the vital K4 square, and at the same time it invites White to push his pawn to Q5, thereby relieving the tension in the centre.

So White now has to choose between blocking the centre with P–Q5 (which, after all, has the advantage of gaining space for White) and exchanging off pawns in the centre with expectations of establishing a strongly placed Knight either on Q5 or on KB5.

105

**Line 1A**

| *13.* P–Q5 | N–Q1 |
|---|---|

Here the Knight does get in the way of Black's pieces and prevents the co-operation of the Rooks; but Black hopes to remedy this by playing his N–N2 or to KB2 (after reorganizing his Kingside).

### *14.* P–QR4

A strong move that threatens to win a pawn by P × P and thus puts pressure on Black's Queen-side.

This variation does retain quite a lot of initiative for White, as was shown in a famous game won by Capablanca over Vidmar at New York, 1927, which continued *14.* ..., P–N5 (better is *14.* ..., R–N1; though White still has the better of it after *15.* P–QN4, N–N2; *16.* RP × P, RP × P; *17.* N–B1).

*15.* N–B4, P–QR4; *16.* KN × P (a fine combination that gives White a won ending).

*16.* ..., B–R3; *17.* B–N3, P × N; *18.* P–Q6, B × P; *19.* Q × B, Q × Q; *20.* N × Q, N–N2; *21.* N × N, B × N; *22.* P × P, BP × P; *23.* P–B3, KR–Q1; *24.* B–K3, P–R3; *25.* KR–Q1, B–B3; *26.* QR–B1, B–K1; *27.* K–B2, R × R; *28.* R × R, R–B1; *29.* P–N4, B–Q2; *30.* B–N6, B–K3; *31.* B × B, P × B; *32.* R–Q8 ch, R × R; *33.* B × R, N–Q2; *34.* B × P, N–B4; *35.* P–N3, N × NP; *36.* B × P, N–Q5; *37.* P–R5, resigns. Black must give

up the Knight for the QRP – a game that merits a lot of study
and that shows the power of the Ruy Lopez opening to the full.

*Line 1B* (see Diagram 105)

> *13.* P × BP

This, the modern line, gives the game a much more open ten-
dency; that is to say, the pieces can move more freely in the
centre.

| | |
|---|---|
| *13.* ... | P × P |
| *14.* N–B1 | |

White directs the Knight towards an outpost on either Q5 or B5
via K3.

| | |
|---|---|
| *14.* ... | B–Q3 |
| *15.* P–QR4 | |

Again we have the threat of **P × P**.

| | |
|---|---|
| *15.* ... | R–N1 |
| *16.* B–N5 | N–K1 |

Not liking *17.* B × N, P × B; when his King-side would be badly
broken.

| | |
|---|---|
| *17.* P × P | P × P |
| *18.* N–K3 | P–B3 |
| *19.* N–Q5 | Q–B2 |
| *20.* B–K3 | |

With advantage to White.

The game Kavalek–Filip, Wijk-aan-Zee, 1970, now continued
*20.* ..., N–K2; *21.* R–R7, R–N2; *22.* R × R, B × R; *23.*
N–N6, N–B1; *24.* N × N, B × N; *25.* N–R4, and White retains
his hold on the position.

*Line 2* (see Diagram 104)

> *12.* ...            BP × P

An energetic idea that aims at trying for counter-play along the
QB file.

| | |
|---|---|
| *13.* P × P | N–B3 |
| *14.* N–N3 | P–QR4 |
| *15.* B–K3 | P–R5 |
| *16.* QN–Q2 | B–K3 |
| *17.* P–R3 | |

Apparently failing to take advantage of Black's blunder by *17.* P–Q5, but to this Black can well reply *17.* ..., N–QN5 with a double attack on White's Bishop.

| | |
|---|---|
| *17.* ... | N–QR4 |
| *18.* B–Q3 | Q–N1 |
| *19.* Q–K2 | |

And White has a clear advantage.

A game, Adorjan versus Radio Listeners, Hungary, 1978, continued *19.* ..., B–Q2; *20.* KR–QB1, R–K1; *21.* QR–N1, P–R3; *22.* P–QN4, P × P e.p.; *23.* N × NP, P–Q4; *24.* N × P, B × QRP; *25.* N–B5, and White has a winning position.

*Line 3* (see Diagram 104)

| | |
|---|---|
| *12.* ... | B–Q2 |

Black completes his development and, given time, will be able to launch a counter-attack.

| | |
|---|---|
| *13.* N–B1 | KR–K1 |
| *14.* P–QN3 | |

A good move that prevents Black from playing N–B5 and prepares to develop the QB along the long diagonal (QR1–KR8).

| | |
|---|---|
| *14.* ... | P–N3 |

Preparing in his turn to play B–KB1 and B–N2. If he plays at once *14.* ..., B–KB1; then White can disturb this sequence of moves by replying *15.* B–N5.

| | |
|---|---|
| *15.* B–N5 | |

Now that Black has weakened his King-side, White plays to

exchange off Bishops and thus leave Black weak on the black squares.

|       |          |
|-------|----------|
| 15. ... | N–R4 |
| 16. B × B | R × B |
| 17. N–K3 | |

Threatening N–Q5 and thus forcing back the enemy Knight.

|       |          |
|-------|----------|
| 17. ... | N–KB3 |
| 18. R–QB1 | |

So that if now Black plays 18. ..., BP × P; 19. P × P will threaten a discovered attack on (see page1 59) the Black Queen.

The game Stein–Matanovic, Tel Aviv Olympiad, 1964, continued here 18. ..., N–N2; 19. P–QN4, P–B5; 20. P–QR4, QR–K1; 21. RP × P, RP × P; 22. R–R1, B–B3; 23. R–R6, Q–B1; 24. P–Q5, and White had the advantage.

*Line 4* (see Diagram 104)

|       |          |
|-------|----------|
| 12. ... | R–Q1 |

An aggressive, if somewhat artificial, continuation that plans a counter-attack in the centre by P–Q4.

|       |          |
|-------|----------|
| 13. N–B1 | P–Q4 |
| 14. P × KP | P × P |
| 15. N(B1)–Q2 | |

15. N(B3)–Q2, would be bad on account of 15. ..., Q × P; 16. B × P, N × B; 17. R × N, Q × R when Black wins.

|       |          |
|-------|----------|
| 15. ... | P × N |
| 16. P × N | B × P |
| 17. Q × P | B–K3 |

White still has the better game after 17. ..., B–N2; B–K4.

|       |          |
|-------|----------|
| 18. N–K4 | B–K2 |
| 19. Q–R5 | P–N3 |
| 20. Q–R6 | |

With much the better game for White.

## THE QUEEN'S GAMBIT

All the openings we have looked at so far have been King's Pawn openings; that is to say, they have started with *1*. P–K4. But there is also a very large section of openings that are classified as Queen's Pawn openings, and these commence with *1*. P–Q4. Of these, the most important, the oldest and the most popular is the Queen's Gambit which, like all sound openings, is largely concerned with the control of the centre. White brings pressure to bear on Black's Q4 so as to induce him to exchange off the QP for the QBP. Once this has been achieved, White is able to occupy the central point on K4 as well as that on Q4, and then he has a jumping-off point for all kinds of attack on the opponent's King.

| | |
|---|---|
| *1*. P–Q4 | P–Q4 |
| *2*. P–QB4 | P–K3 |

This is one of the steadiest and safest ways of defending the Queen's Gambit. Black's pawn chain is sound and solid and, at the same time, he gives developing possibilities to his KB and also to his Queen. It has, however, the drawback of shutting in the QB, and Black has to spend much time in getting this piece into action.

Naturally, Black can also give up all attempts at holding the central point on Q4 and accept the gambit with *2*. . . ., P × P. This is quite a feasible line as I hope to show in Chapter 7; but acceptance of the Gambit pawn does not mean that Black should try to hold on to it at all costs. If he does so attempt, then he can get a bad position by, for instance *2*. . . ., P × P; *3*. N–KB3, P–QN4; *4*. P–K3, P–QB3; *5*. P–QR4, B–N2; *6*. P × P, P × P; *7*. P–QN3, Q–B1; *8*. P × P, P × P; *9*. Q–R4 ch, N–B3; *10*. B × P, and White regains his pawn with much the better position (he controls the centre, is better developed and threatens eventually to get a Rook on the QB file, after which Black's Queen will be most uncomfortably placed.)

*3*. N–QB3

Putting some pressure on the enemy QP and at the same time ideally developing the Knight which now exerts some control also on K4.

3. ...          N–KB3

By the same token Black's Knight is admirably placed both for defence and for counter-attack (it sometimes can go to K5 with effect).

    4. B–N5

Again putting pressure (indirectly this time) on Black's Q4.

4. ...          B–K2

Here Black could also play, if he so wishes, 4. ..., QN–Q2; when White must not fall for the trap 5. P × P, P × P; 6. N × P, since then he would lose a piece after 6. ..., N × N; 7. B × Q, B–N5 ch; 8. Q–Q2, K × B; etc.

5. P–K3          O–O

Black has got himself castled long before White and this is due to White's preoccupation with the Queen's wing and with the pressure he is exerting there.

Here it should be observed that White cannot have everything and that in any case it does not take him long to set matters right and develop his own King-side pieces.

6. N–B3          QN–Q2
7. R–B1

Again White works on the problem of getting Black to relinquish his support for the QP. The Rook is placed on the QB file in readiness for taking advantage of Black's P × P, and many games have been settled by White's QR seizing control of the QB file.

7. ...          P–B3

Black continues to buttress his Q4 square.

    8. B–Q3

Or White may play 8. Q–B2 and then continue to tease and tempt Black with the objective of getting him to yield his control

118

of Q4. Black could reply 8. ..., P–QR3 and if then White himself played 9. P–QR3, Black could reply 9. ..., R–K1.

But let us return to the main line of the Classical Defence.

| 8. ... | P × P |
| 9. B × P | N–Q4 |

An interesting manoeuvre introduced by the great Capablanca. The idea is to exchange off a number of pieces and then free his QB by playing P–K4.

| 10. B × B | Q × B |
| 11. O–O | N × N |

More exchanges.

| 12. R × N | P–K4 |

At last he has advanced this pawn so that it does not impede the development of his own QB. But White's initiative is by no means exhausted.

106

Of the many moves at White's disposal here, perhaps the best is

| 13. Q–B2 | P × P |

Keeping rigorously to his plan of clearing the lines in the centre.

| 14. P × P | N–N3 |
| 15. R–K3 | |

A strong move that gives him control of the centre K file and, even more important, control of the K5 square.

| | |
|---|---|
| 15. ... | Q–B3 |
| 16. B–N3 | B–N5 |
| 17. KR–K1 | QR–Q1 |
| 18. Q–B5 | Q–Q3 |
| 19. P–KR3 | B × N |
| 20. R × B | Q × Q |
| 21. P × Q | |

And White has the upper hand.

107

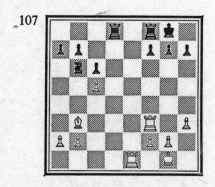

Here the game, Gligoric–Drimer, Hastings, 1970/71, continued 21. ..., N–Q2; 22. R–K7, N × P; 23. B × P ch, with a winning game for White. Instead, Black should have played 21. ..., N–B1; when White's advantage, though still there after 22. R–K4, P–KN3; 23. R(K4)–KB4, R–Q2; 24. R–B6, is not so marked.

In fact, Black's disadvantage is so clear in this classical line that it is rarely played nowadays. Most players go for the temporizing lines involving small pawn moves or centralizing Rook moves. That these also have their dangers is shown by the following brief game which was played in Mexico in 1978.

WHITE: SHAMKOVICH        BLACK: ANGUIANO

*1.* P–Q4, P–Q4; *2.* P–QB4, P–K3; *3.* N–QB3, N–KB3; *4.* B–N5, QN–Q2; *5.* P–K3, B–K2; *6.* N–B3, O–O; *7.* R–B1, P–B3; *8.* Q–B2, R–K1; *9.* P–QR3, P–KR3; (better is P–QN3) *10.* B–B4, P × P; *11.* B × BP, P–QN4; *12.* B–R2, B–N2; *13.* O–O, Q–N3; *14.* N–K5, KR–Q1; *15.* B × RP, P × B; *16.* B × P, N × N; (if *16.* ..., P × B; *17.* Q–N6 ch, K–R1; *18.* N–B7 mate) *17.* P × N, N–Q4; *18.* Q–N6 ch, K–R1; *19.* Q × P ch, resigns. Because of *19.* ..., K–N1; *20.* Q–N6 ch, K–R1; *21.* B × P, P–B4; *22.* P–K6, N–B3; *23.* Q–R6 ch, N–R2; *24.* B–N6 and mates.

## EXERCISES

**1.** How should White play after *1.* P–K4, P–K4; *2.* N–KB3, P–KB3?

108

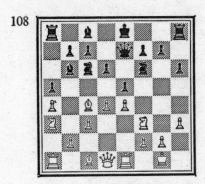

Black to play

**2.** Is N–Q1 a good move for Black in this position? If not, then what is?

3.   Why not, after *1.* P–K4, P–K4; *2.* P–KB4, P × P; *3.* N–KB3, P–KN4; *4.* P–KR4, defend the pawn attacked by 4.   ..., P–KR3?

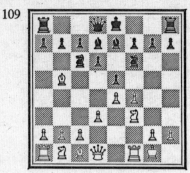

109

White to play

4.   In this position, can one win a pawn by *7.* B × N, B × B; *8.* P × P, P × P; *9.* N × P?

5.   Can White win a pawn after *1.* P–K4, P–K4; *2.* N–KB3, N–QB3; *3.* B–N5, P–QR3?

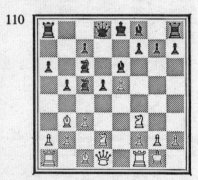

110

Black to play

6.   Is P–N3 a good move here? If not, suggest a better one.

7. What should White play after *1*. P–K4, P–K4; *2*. N–KB3, N–QB3; *3*. B–N5, P–QR3; *4*. B–R4, N–B3; *5*. O–O, B–K2; and why?

111

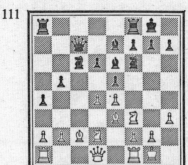

White to play

8. Can White win a piece in this position by P–Q5?

112

Black to play

9. Why is N–R4 a bad move here for Black?

10. After *1*. P–Q4, P–Q4; *2*. P–QB4, P–K3; *3*. N–QB3, N–KB3; *4*. B–N5, QN–Q2; can White win a pawn by *5*. P × P, P × P; *6*. N × P?

## ANSWERS TO THE EXERCISES

1. White should play 3. N × P, and if then 3. ..., P × N; 4. Q–R5 ch, when 4. ..., P–N3; 5. Q × KP ch, loses a Rook for Black; whilst still worse for him would be 4. ..., K–K2; 5. Q × P ch, K–B2; 6. B–B4 ch, etc.

2. (see Diagram 108) No, it is a bad move; better is O–O.

3. Because of 5. P × P, when 5. ..., P × P loses the Rook.

4. (see Diagram 109) No, because of Q–Q5 ch, winning the Knight.

5. No, since after 4. B × N, QP × B; 5. N × P, Q–Q5; and Black wins back his pawn.

6. (see Diagram 110) P–N3 is a bad move; better is P–Q5.

7. After 6. ..., O–O; Black was threatening N × P; so the KP should be protected by R–K1 (or by N–B3 or by P–Q3).

8. (see Diagram 111) No, because Black replies N–QN5.

9. (see Diagram 112) Because after 1. ..., N–R4 there would come 2. P × P, KP × P; 3. N × P, and if then 3. ..., P × N; 4. B–B7, winning the Queen.

10. Yes, indeed he can win a pawn by 5. P × P, P × P; 6. N × P, but he loses a piece then after 6. ..., N × N; 7. B × Q, B–N5 ch; 8. Q–Q2, K × B; etc.

# CHAPTER 7

# HOW TO DEFEND WITH BLACK

In the previous chapter we have looked at the openings chiefly from White's point of view. The main problem was how to develop an attack, and we only considered what Black was to do in reply to this.

However, by and large you will get as many Blacks as you get Whites in the course of a sufficiently long period of playing chess, and it is just as essential to know how to defend as to know how to attack. In any case, basically the problem of development remains the same, whether you have the White pieces or the Black. The pieces still have to be brought out and the question of control of the centre has to be borne in mind. This means that only those openings for Black that fulfil these two requirements come into consideration.

But there is one further consideration that must be rigorously kept in mind when you have Black, a consideration that is not nearly so important when you have White. Your defence must be such that it allows you as soon as possible to go over to the counter-attack. Defences that do not permit this are passive defences, and very few passive defences ever succeed in their aim.

Again we have to divide the field into two here, according to whether White opens with *1*. P–K4 or with *1*. P–Q4. Against *1*. P–K4, we have what is known as the Half-Open Defences; by Half-Open is meant lines that refrain from opening up the centre at the beginning of play but gradually (more rapidly in some cases than in others) open up the centre as play proceeds. There are quite a number of these, but undoubtedly the two most popular (and probably the two best) are the Sicilian Defence and the French Defence.

## THE SICILIAN DEFENCE

This is a very old defence whose origins are lost in the mists of time, and it has always enjoyed much popularity – rightly so, since it is the best example of a counter-attack on the centre among all the openings.

*1.* P–K4                          P–QB4

From the very first move there exists a clear and vigorous counter-threat in the centre. Black attacks White's Q4 and also sets up a potential outpost in the centre for his QN on Q5. At the same time he sets up some development squares for his Queen, on QB2 where it controls the central point K4, or on QN3 where it reinforces the attack on White's Q4 and also attacks a vulnerable point in White's pawn formation, his QN2, or on QR4 where it indirectly attacks the enemy King.

*2.* N–KB3

White hastens to deal with the threat on his Q4 and himself plans to gain command of the centre with P–Q4.

*2.* ...                          P–Q3

Linking up the pawns and thereby giving each pawn added strength. He also allows for the development of his QB and protects the central K4 square.

*3.* P–Q4

The battle for the centre commences.

*3.* ...                          P × P

Black's game becomes constricted if he allows White to play P–Q5, and in any case he is hoping for counter-play along the half-open QB file.

*4.* N × P

And not *4.* Q × P, when Black would develop his QN to QB3 with gain of time owing to the attack on White's Queen.

*4.* ...                          N–KB3

But Black can and does develop with gain of time by attacking the enemy KP.

5. N–QB3     P–KN3

The Bishop is to be developed on KN2 where it is ideally placed to exert pressure along the long diagonal. In so doing, it co-operates with the entire action of the Black forces so far, which consists of an attack on the central black squares.

This type of development of the Bishop on either KN2 or QN2 is known as a fianchetto, from the Italian *fiancata* which means moves played on the side or flank. We shall see its use in other openings, notably in the King's Indian Defence, page 140.

The whole line for Black is called the Dragon variation, possibly because of the fancied resemblance of Black's pawn chain to the outline of a dragon.

113
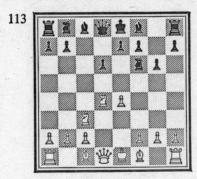

White to play

White has three main methods of pursuing the game. One is that of pawn attack by 6. P–B4 and the other two are solid developing moves such as B–K3 or B–K2.

*Line 1*

6. P–B4

A fierce attacking move that threatens to break up Black's

position by P–K5. In order to defeat this plan, Black must bend all his efforts towards controlling his K4 square.

     6.  ...                   QN–Q2

And not 6. ..., N–B3 when White can still force through P–K5 by playing 7. N × N, P × N; 8. P–K5.

     7. B–K2                 B–N2
     8. B–K3                 O–O
     9. B–B3                 N–N3

Clearing the diagonal for the development of his QB and threatening to embarrass White by N–B5. White takes immediate steps to deal with the Knight threat.

    10. Q–K2               P–K4
    11. N–N3

114

Black to play

This is the position attained in a game, Tolush–Abramian, Leningrad, 1939. White seems to have the advantage since he has developed all his pieces, whereas Black's QB is still at home. But he has not yet castled as Black has, and an analysis by the British grandmaster, Raymond Keene, shows an ingenious method by which Black may exploit the fact that White's King is still uncastled: 11. ..., N–N5; 12. B × N, (if 12. O–O–O,

N × B; *13*. Q × N, B–R3; *14*. P–N3, Q–B3 and White cannot defend his KB4) *12*. ..., Q–R5 ch; *13*. P–N3, Q × B; *14*. Q × Q, B × Q; and Black has a good game. For if now *15*. B × N, P × B; *16*. N–Q5, P × P; *17*. P × P, B × P and the Bishop now has a wonderful reach right along the long diagonal.

From this you can realize how strong the fianchettoed KB can become.

*Line 2* (see Diagram 113)

> 6. B–K3

Here the Bishop is beautifully placed. The fact that it is in the centre means it is ready to attack on both wings. Moreover, White can play Q–Q2 and bring these two pieces into most effective co-operation with the threat in mind of B–R6.

Naturally, Q–Q2 can be played only after the centre has been buttressed by P–B3. For sooner or later it will become necessary to ward off Black's N–KN5. Black cannot do it at once since 6. ..., N–N5 would be met by 7. B–N5 ch, which, as a moment's thought will show, wins a piece.

So

> 6. ...                                    B–N2
> 7. P–B3

White could also play B–K2 but as this usually transposes to the *6.* B–K2 line it needs no special treatment here.

> 7. ...                                    N–B3
> 8. Q–Q2                                   O–O
> 9. B–QB4

Here the Bishop attacks Black's KB2 which, as I have already pointed out in other openings, is a weak point in the enemy camp.

> 9. ...                                    B–Q2

Black calmly continues his development, and now White has to make up his mind: is he going to castle Queen-side and then go in for an all-out attack against Black's King, or will he castle King-side and content himself with a quiet and normal position?

> *10.* O–O–O

In fact, unless something attacking is played here, White will lose all initiative and the enterprise in the game will pass over to Black.

> *10.* ...                                     Q–R4

Black too must counter-attack as soon as possible and with the utmost vigour.

> *11.* B–N3

This consolidates the position on the Queen-side and averts Black playing R–QB1 with a veiled attack on the Bishop.

> *11.* ...                                     KR–QB1

Black plays the Rook move anyway and this is, as it happens, his best move.

> *12.* P–KR4

White embarks on an all-out attack against the enemy King.

> *12.* ...                                     N–K4

A good double-purpose move. The Knight gives added protection to the King-side whilst at the same time threatening to go to QB5 to attack the White Queen.

Note that much of the strength of this move lies in the fact that it *centralizes* the Knight.

> *13.* P–R5

A pawn sacrifice to open up lines of attack – and a dangerous one.

> *13.* ...                                     N ×RP

Better than P × P which would horribly break up Black's King-side pawn formation.

> *14.* P–N4                               N–KB3

And not *14.* ..., N–N6; *15.* R–R3 when the Knight would be lost.

*15.* B–R6

Threatening *16.* B × B, K × B; *17.* Q–R6 ch, K–N1; *18.* N–Q5, with a winning attack on the King. In view of this alarming threat, Black must do something vigorous and, since by playing the KR to the QB file he has prepared for this eventuality, he is now in a position to counter-attack with the utmost vigour.

115

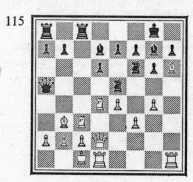

Black to play

*15.* ...                         R × N

A typical counter-stroke that interferes with the smooth flow of White's attack and gives the initiative to Black. It is true that giving up the Rook for the Knight (or sacrificing the exchange, as this manoeuvre is known) involves surrendering a piece of greater value for the Knight (for the respective value of pieces see Chapter 8, page 169); but in return Black breaks up White's pawn formation and also upsets the working of White's game as the first player has planned it out.

*16.* P × R

If *16.* Q × R, Q × Q; *17.* P × Q, B × B ch; *18.* R × B, N–R4

131

(trapping the Rook); *19.* P × N, K–N2; winning the Rook, and getting the advantage.

| | |
|---|---|
| *16.* ... | B × B |
| *17.* R × B | R–QB1 |
| *18.* K–N2 | Q–N3 |

Threatening to win the Queen by N–B5 ch.

| | |
|---|---|
| *19.* Q–R2 | Q–B4 |
| *20.* R × P | |

Another lively move; the idea is that if *20.* ..., N × R; *21.* R–KR1, with a mating attack.

| | |
|---|---|
| *20.* ... | Q × P ch |
| *21.* K–N1 | N × R |
| *22.* R–R1 | P–K3 |

So as to give the King an outlet on K2.

| | |
|---|---|
| *23.* Q × N ch | K–B1 |
| *24.* Q–R6 ch | K–K2 |
| *25.* Q–N5 ch | P–B3 |
| *26.* R–R7 ch | N–B2 |
| *27.* Q × P | Q–K8 ch |

And the game is a draw by perpetual check.

*Line 3* (see Diagram 113)

     6. B–K2

A quiet but solid developing move. White hastens to castle King-side and then proceed with an attack on that wing.

| | |
|---|---|
| *6.* ... | B–N2 |
| *7.* O–O | O–O |
| *8.* N–N3 | |

To prevent Black from freeing his position in the centre by P–Q4. If, for example, *8.* P–B3, N–B3; *9.* B–K3, P–Q4 with full equality.

| | |
|---|---|
| *8.* ... | N–B3 |
| *9.* K–R1 | |

An idea stemming from the then world champion, Alexander

Alekhine; it prepares a pawn storm on the King-side by tucking the King away in safety in the corner, and at the same time it avoids any trouble with the Black Queen darting out to QN3 and counter-attacking on the weak point (weak for both White and Black) on KB2.

| 9. ... | P–QR4 |

Vigorous counter-attack; Black is ready to thrust this pawn right down to R6 where it helps the fianchettoed Bishop in its attack along the diagonal. White at once takes steps to stop this thrust.

| 10. P–QR4 | B–K3 |
| 11. P–B4 | Q–N3 |

Black concentrates on the weakness on White's QN4.

Playing against Alekhine at Montevideo in 1939, I tried *11. ...,* Q–B1 here with the idea of playing an eventual B–N5; but, after *12.* B–K3, B–N5; *13.* B–N1, R–Q1; *14.* N–Q5, B × B; *15.* Q × B, N × N; *16.* P × N, N–N5; *17.* P–B4, Q–B2; *18.* N–Q4, White, threatening P–B5, had the better game.

116

White to play

| 12. P–B5 | B × N |
| 13. P × B | Q–N5 |
| 14. B–QB4 | N–K4 |

With a level game.

In all these lines the power of Black's fianchettoed Bishop, backed up by aggressive play on the Queen's wing, gives Black excellent chances.

A good example of all this is the following game, played at Decin in Czechoslovakia, 1979.

WHITE: R. TISCHBIEREK          BLACK: L. GAZIK

*1*. P–K4, P–QB4; *2*. N–KB3, P–Q3; *3*. P–Q4, P × P; *4*. N × P, N–KB3; *5*. N–QB3, P–KN3; *6*. B–K2, B–N2; *7*. O–O, O–O; thus far as in Line 3. Now White tries an interesting variation from the normal with *8*. B–KN5, N–B3; *9*. N–N3, P–QR3; *10*. P–QR4, B–K3; *11*. P–B4 (better was *11*. K–R1); *11*. . . ., P–N4; *12*. P × P, Q–N3 ch; *13*. K–R1, P × P; *14*. R × R, R × R; *15*. N–Q5 (if *15*. B × P, N × P!); *15*. . . ., B × N; *16*. P × B, N–QR4; *17*. N × N, R × N; *18*. B–B3, (preferable is *18*. P–B3); *18*. . . ., P–N5; *19*. R–K1, P–R3; *20*. B–R4, Q–N4; *21*. R × P, N × P; *22*. B × N, Q × B; *23*. Q–K1, Q–B5; *24*. R–N7, Q–R3 (threatening R–R8); *25*. R–N8 ch, K–R2; White resigns. Either he loses his Queen or he is mated.

## THE FRENCH DEFENCE

Rather less popular than the Sicilian but still widely played and with a long and, on the whole, successful history, this defence, like all good and sound defences, is based on a struggle for the centre – as you will soon see.

| | |
|---|---|
| *1*. P–K4 | P–K3 |
| *2*. P–Q4 | P–Q4 |

At once Black challenges White's control of the central K4 square. If you look at the pawn formation, you will see first of all that the challenge is a direct one and that it cannot be ignored by White. You will also see that, while Black's KB is given considerable scope for development, his QB is the Cinderella of the piece and has been shut in, seemingly for good, by one of its own pawns. In this, as in so many defences with the Black pieces, lies the one great drawback. In fact, it is not too much to say that, once you have solved the problem of the development of the QB; you have really solved all problems of defence.

White can react to Black's challenge in three very different ways. He can exchange off pawns (a simplifying manoeuvre which should set Black few problems and with which I will deal later); or he can protect and maintain his pawn on K4 by either N–QB3 or N–Q2; or, finally, he can advance the pawn to K5.

In reply to this advance variation, Black gets a good game by attacking the base of White's advanced centre. After *3*. P–K5, he should play P–QB4 and then proceed to attack White's Q4 square with all the forces at his command: by N–QB3, Q–N3 and even eventually by either P–KB3 or N–K2 (or R3) and then by N–B4.

Let us first look at the most important line, which is concerned with the maintenance of the pawn on K4.

> *3*. N–QB3

Black frees his game quite markedly after *3*. N–Q2 with *3*. ..., P–QB4.

> *3*. ...                    B–N5

Known as the Winawer Variation after a great Polish master of the late nineteenth century, this is the very essence of counter-attack. White can reply by advancing his KP or by exchanging off pawns. Let us look at the first line, which is the main line.

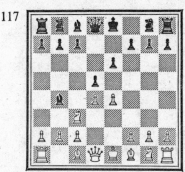

117

White to play

> 4. P–K5                    P–QB4

In all these advance lines it is the very best idea for Black to attack the pawn base in this fashion since, if he succeeds in undermining it, then the strategic battle is already won.

| | |
|---|---|
| 5. P–QR3 | B × N ch |
| 6. P × B | N–K2 |

And now White has to choose between the solid developing line 7. N–B3 and the more violent 7. Q–N4.

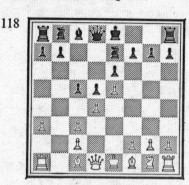

118

White to play

*Line 1*

| | |
|---|---|
| 7. N–B3 | QN–B3 |
| 8. B–Q3 | |

Against 8. P–QR4, with the idea of playing B–R3, Black plays 8. . . ., Q–R4; 9. B–Q2, P–B5.

| | |
|---|---|
| 8. . . . | Q–R4 |
| 9. O–O | P–B5 |

Capturing the BP is too dangerous: e.g. 9. . . ., Q × BP; 10. B–Q2, Q–N7; 11. R–N1, Q × RP; 12. R–N3, Q–R7 (or 12. . . ., Q–R5; 13. B–QN5); 13. Q–B1, P–B5; 14. R–R3, and the Black Queen is lost.

10. B–K2

But now the pawn can be taken.

|        |             |
|--------|-------------|
| 10. ... | Q × BP     |
| 11. B–Q2 | Q–N7      |
| 12. R–N1 | Q × RP    |
| 13. R–R1 |           |

And White can force a draw, but no more, by chasing the Queen continually.

*Line 2* (see Diagram 118)

|           |        |
|-----------|--------|
| 7. Q–N4   | Q–B2   |

With indirect counter-threats on White's QB3.

|            |        |
|------------|--------|
| 8. Q × NP  | R–N1   |
| 9. Q × RP  | P × P  |
| 10. N–K2   | QN–B3  |
| 11. P–KB4  | B–Q2   |
| 12. Q–Q3   | P × P  |

and Black, whose position is nice and compact, has certainly not got the worse of it.

*The Exchange Variation*

I pointed out at the beginning of my piece on the French Defence that White could exchange off pawns on move 3 but that this would get him nowhere. This equally applies to the Exchange Variation of the Winawer, and play is similar.

|            |        |
|------------|--------|
| 1. P–K4    | P–K3   |
| 2. P–Q4    | P–Q4   |
| 3. N–QB3   | B–N5   |
| 4. P × P   | P × P  |
| 5. B–Q3    | N–QB3  |

The most aggressive move; but he could also play here 5. ..., N–K2.

|           |        |
|-----------|--------|
| 6. P–QR3  |        |

Putting the question to the Bishop – either to exchange off for the Knight, or to retire the piece to R4 or K2.

|        |          |
|--------|----------|
| 6. ... | B × N ch |
| 7. P × B | N–KB3  |

After 7. ..., KN–K2; White has a dangerous attack by 8. Q–R5.

|          |          |
|----------|----------|
| 8. B–KN5 | Q–K2 ch  |

Better than 8. ..., O–O when White will play 9. N–K2 and have the makings of a fine King-side attack. In this variation Black must be prepared to play O–O–O.

|          |        |
|----------|--------|
| 9. N–K2  | B–Q2   |
| 10. O–O  | P–KR3  |

119

White to play

|          |        |
|----------|--------|
| 11. B × N | Q × B |
| 12. Q–Q2  | O–O–O |

And the position is level. By this, I mean that the player who knows best how to manoeuvre in this position will gain the upper hand.

An object lesson in handling such positions was provided by fourteen-year-old Nigel Short in the 1979 British Championship at Chester. In play with the Black pieces against the well-known grandmaster, Tony Miles, he had the position shown in Diagram 119, in which Miles made the mistake of playing *11*. B–KB4, and play proceeded *11*. ..., O–O–O; *12*. P–QB4, B–K3; *13*. P–B5, P–KN4; *14*. B–Q2, N–K5; *15*. R–N1, P–B4; *16*. P–KB3, N × B; *17*. Q × N, P–B5; establishing a hold on K6 of which he takes fine advantage later on. Note that Black's operations are based on the centre.

*18*. B–N5, B–Q2; *19*. KR–K1, Q–B3; *20*. Q–B3, QR–K1; Black proceeds to occupy the vital K6 square.

*21*. Q–N3, R–K6; *22*. B–Q3, and not *22*. Q × P, B–K3; when the White Queen is lost.

*22*. ..., N–Q1; *23*. P–B4, B–B4; *24*. B × B ch, Q × B; *25*. Q–R2, KR–K1; *26*. R–N2, P–N5; *27*. R–KB1, NP × P; *28*. NP × P, R–N1 ch; *29*. K–R1, Q–R6; *30*. R–KB2, R × BP; *31*. N–N1, R–K6; *32*. R–N2 (if *32*. N × Q, Black mates by R–K8 ch etc).

*32*. ..., Q–K3; *33*. R × R, Q × R; *34*. P × P, P–B6; *35*. P–Q6, Q–N4; *36*. P–Q7 ch; Black was threatening R–K8.

*36*. ..., K × P; *37*. Q–N1, N–K3; *38*. Q–R7 ch, K–B3; *39*. Q–B7, N × QP; *40*. Q–QB4, Q × P; *41*. Q–R4 ch, P–N4; *42*. Q–Q1, Q–Q4; *43*. R–KB2, R–K7; the death-blow, and a neat one.

*44*. Q–B1 ch, K–N2; *45*. N × R, P × N dis ch; *46*. R–N2, N–B7; White resigns.

### THE QUEEN-SIDE DEFENCES

So far we have been discussing the defences to *1*. P–K4. But equally important, especially in the last fifty years, are Black's defences to *1*. P–Q4. There are a very large number of such defences; but, of them all, two in particular have emerged as the most frequently and successfully used during the period that commenced with the end of the First World War: the King's Indian Defence and the Nimzo-Indian Defence. Each, in a different way, is based on a counter-attack; whilst the Nimzo-Indian started off by being the more popular, it has since been overhauled and passed by the King's Indian, which is now the chief defence to the Queen's Pawn.


### THE KING'S INDIAN DEFENCE

*1.* P–Q4                                    N–KB3

Indian defences are so called because the move *1.* ..., N–KB3 was popular in India in the early nineteenth century.

*2.* P–QB4                                  P–KN3

Black decides to fianchetto his KB and it is this move which makes it a King's Indian. If, for example, he had played *2.* ..., P–QN3 the defence would have been a Queen's Indian.

The principal aim of the King's Indian Defence is, by the aid of the KB, to counter-attack White on the black squares of the diagonal on which the KB is placed. That is to say, the counter-attack is made on the long diagonal stretching from Black's KR1 to his QR8. Though this attack is made, in the first instance, on White's Queen-side pawns, it is a curious fact that the strategy for White is to pursue an attack on the Queen-side and for Black to attack on the King-side, as will soon appear.

White has now to choose between two very different lines. He can either concentrate on ordinary piece development with *3.* N–QB3, or else he can imitate Black's fianchetto development with *3.* P–KN3. Divergent though these lines are, it should be noted that both are concerned with putting pressure on the central white squares.

*Line 1*

*3.* N–QB3                                  B–N2
*4.* P–K4

Occupying the centre and threatening to chase away the enemy Knight by *5.* P–K5.

*4.* ...                                     P–Q3

Preventing White's P–K5 which would now be met by *5.* ...,

P × P; 6. P × P, Q × Q ch; 7. N × Q, KN–Q2; 8. P–B4, P–KB3 with advantage to Black.

>    5. P–B3

Of the many moves at his disposal (5. P–B4, 5. N–KB3, 5. P–KN3, etc.) this is the most solid, since it gains an iron control of White's central K4 square. It is known as the Sämisch Variation, after the West German grandmaster, Fritz Sämisch, who introduced a number of original opening ideas.

120

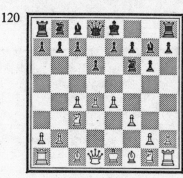

Black to play

>    5. ...                          O–O
>    6. B–K3

A good developing move, since White can follow it up with Q–Q2, aiming at the exchange of the fianchettoed Bishop by B–R6.

>    6. ...                          P–K4

Black may also play 6. ..., N–B3; but this line is a bit too complicated for the less advanced player.

>    7. P–Q5

Or he may play 7. KN–K2, to which Black replies 7. ..., P–B3.

>    7. ...                          P–B3

Black foresees that White is going to castle Queen-side, and therefore opens up lines of attack on that wing.

>    8. Q–Q2

Or he may play 8. KN–K2, when Black proceeds, as in the main line, with P × P.

>    8. ...                           P × P
>    9. BP × P                        P–QR3

Preparing an attack by P–QN4.

>    10. O–O–O                        QN–Q2
>    11. K–N1

White tucks away his King into comparative safety, away from the open file.

>    11. ...                          P–QN4
>    12. P–KN4                        N–B4
>    13. R–B1

13. P–N5, N–R4 would block White's attempts at attack.

>    13. ...                          N–K1

Preparing a typical counter-thrust in the King's Indian: P–B4.

>    14. P–KR4                        P–B4
>    15. NP × P                       P × P
>    16. B–N5                         B–B3
>    17. P–N4                         N–Q2

And the game is level.

*Line 2*

>    1. P–Q4                          N–KB3
>    2. P–QB4                         P–KN3
>    3. P–KN3

Quieter than Line 1 but still with the strong strategic idea of using his KB to control the white squares.

| | |
|---|---|
| 3. ... | B–N2 |
| 4. B–N2 | O–O |
| 5. N–QB3 | P–Q3 |
| 6. N–B3 | N–B3 |

Black plans to increase his pressure on the black central squares with P–K4.

| | |
|---|---|
| 7. O–O | P–K4 |
| 8. P–Q5 | |

8. P × P, P × P merely leads to an early draw.

| | |
|---|---|
| 8. ... | N–K2 |

The best place for this Knight, since here it can be useful in helping the King-side counter-attack.

| | |
|---|---|
| 9. P–K4 | N–K1 |

Now we get the typical counter-attack for Black along the KB file by P–KB4.

10. N–K1

White brings his KN over to the Queen-side in order to assist the attack there; at the same time he allows his KBP the possibility of moving either to B3 or B4 according to circumstances.

| | |
|---|---|
| 10. ... | P–KB4 |
| 11. N–Q3 | N–KB3 |
| 12. P–B3 | P–KR4 |

And the chances are about even, with Black having the attack on the King-side where he will advance his pawns and mass his pieces, and White doing exactly the same on the Queen's wing.

A good example of this kind of tug-of-war is the following game which was played in a team match at Leipzig in 1979 between players called Csulits and Lenk. The game followed the analysis as above up to Black's twelfth move, when he played 12. ..., P–KR3 (with the idea of advancing his KNP and then placing his Knight on KN3); thereby reaching the position in Diagram 121.

121

White to play

Play continued *13.* P–B5, P–KN4; *14.* P–QN4, N–N3; *15.* P–QR4, R–B2; *16.* P–R5, B–B1; a dual-purpose move: he controls the vital Q3 square and at the same time allows the KR freedom of movement along the King's wing.

*17.* B–QR3, P–R4; *18.* P–N5, P–B5; *19.* Q–N3, P–N5; both sides are pursuing their respective plans with single-minded enthusiasm; but it is Black's plan that has the most teeth.

*20.* NP × P, N × BP; *21.* N × N, P × N; *22.* P–N6. An attractive idea that indeed results in White obtaining two united passed pawns in the centre. Passed pawns are strong because they can advance without let or hindrance from the enemy pawns on their way to the eighth rank where they may be promoted into Queens.

But in this case, the pawns can be blocked, and meanwhile Black is able to get his QR into the game. Better, therefore, would have been *22.* P × QP, or even P–B6.

*22.* ..., RP × P; *23.* RP × P, BP × P; *24* P × QP, B × P; *25.* N–N5, B–K4; blocking the pawns and keeping up the thematic plan of pressure on the black squares.

*26.* B–N2, R × R; *27.* R × R, B × B; *28.* Q × B, B–Q2; *29.* N–Q4, Q–K2; *30.* Q × P, P × P; *31.* B × P, R–N2 ch; *32.* K–R1, Q–K4; the Queen is most beautifully centrally placed here and White's ensuing moves (made under the influence of time pressure) do not help matters; but his position is in any case

144

extremely vulnerable and Black's attack would have broken through sooner or later. The way White now plays, it is sooner rather than later.

*33.* R–R8 ch, K–R2; *34.* N–K6, Q–B6! a deadly move; White is helpless against the many threats.

*35.* N × R, Q × B ch; *36.* K–N1, Q–Q8 ch; *37.* K–N2, B–R6 ch; and White resigns. If *38.* K × B, Q–N5 checkmate, or *38.* K–B2, N–N5 mate.

## THE NIMZO-INDIAN DEFENCE

|  |  |
|---|---|
| *1.* P–Q4 | N–KB3 |
| *2.* P–QB4 | P–K3 |

This move shows that Black is intending to develop his KB along a different diagonal from that chosen in the King's Indian Defence. What he plans to do with his Bishop is, however, just as striking and basic to Black's whole plan of development as the fianchetto he uses in the King's Indian. (Remember that a fianchetto is where you play P–N3 and then develop the Bishop on N2 and along the chief diagonal of the chess-board.)

|  |  |
|---|---|
| *3.* N–QB3 | B–N5 |

It is this move that makes the defence a Nimzo-Indian, so called because it was the great Jewish-Latvian grandmaster, Aron Nimzowitsch, who first evolved the theory of this defence in the early years of the twentieth century, and also because any defence to the Queen's Pawn involving an early N–KB3 is known as an Indian Defence.

The object of the Bishop move is to contest control of White's central K4 square and, given the opportunity, to double White's QP by exchanging off Bishop for Knight and thereby giving Black something to bite on and exploit in the shape of doubled White pawns on the QB file. (Diagram 122.)

White has many possible and likely-looking lines here. He may hit the Bishop by P–QR3, or develop the minor pieces by either *4.* P–K3 or *4.* N–KB3. Or he may play his Queen out to either B2 or N3, or develop his other Knight later by N–K2. I have neither the space nor the time to deal with all these possibilities here, but have chosen two lines that are the most characteristic in their concentration on the centre.

122

White to play

*Line 1*

    *4.* P–K3

Known as the Rubinstein Variation after the great Russo-Jewish master, Rubinstein, this line was all the rage when I was a young grandmaster, but has rather unjustly gone to the old-fashioned textbooks, despite its many virtues. This is not because of any inherent defect in the Rubinstein plan of action, but merely because of the neglect of the Nimzo-Indian as a whole.

The purpose of the pawn move is to give White a solid pawn structure and at the same time allow his KB as much of a chance as possible of being developed with attack on the enemy King.

    *4.* ...                        O–O

One of the advantages of this defence is that Black can get his King castled into safety quite early on.

    *5.* B–Q3                     P–Q4

Both sides develop quickly and firmly.

    *6.* P–QR3                  B × N ch

Obviously there is no point in Black's losing time with *6. ...,* B–Q3 or B–K2.

|     |           |         |
|-----|-----------|---------|
| 7.  | P × B     | P × P   |
| 8.  | B × P     | P–B4    |

An important move by which Black maintains pressure on White's centre and at the same time gives freedom of action to his Queen.

|     |        |        |
|-----|--------|--------|
| 9.  | N–B3   | Q–B2   |

Threatening to discover an attack on the Bishop by **P × P**.

|     |         |         |
|-----|---------|---------|
| 10. | B–K2    | P–QN3   |
| 11. | O–O     | B–N2    |
| 12. | P–QR4   |         |

Planning to play B–R3.

|     |        |        |
|-----|--------|--------|
| 12. | ...    | R–Q1   |

And Black has a good game.

*Line 2* (see Diagram 122)

|     |        |
|-----|--------|
| 4.  | Q–B2   |

Another steady move with which White avoids the doubling of his pawns on the QB file.

|     |        |        |
|-----|--------|--------|
| 4   | ...    | P–B4   |

Now that the Queen has left the Q file and no longer protects the QP, this is a good and vigorous move. The point is that if White's Q was still on Q1, he could now play P–Q5 with effect.

|     |         |        |
|-----|---------|--------|
| 5.  | P × P   | O–O    |

Black need be in no hurry to regain his pawn, but first of all gets his King into safety and mobilizes his KR.

|     |         |         |
|-----|---------|---------|
| 6.  | P–QR3   | B × BP  |
| 7.  | B–B4    | N–B3    |
| 8.  | N–B3    | P–QN3   |
| 9.  | P–K3    | B–N2    |

| 10. B–K2 | B–K2 |
| 11. R–Q1 | R–B1 |

and Black, with his strong Bishop raking White's King-side, has the advantage.

123

White to play

A game, Soos–Hübner, Zonal Tournament, Lucerne, 1979, continued here: *12*. O–O, N–QR4; *13*. N–QN5 (better is *13*. N–Q2).

*13*. ..., B × N; *14*. P × B, P–QR3; *15*. N–Q6, R–B3; *16*. B–K5 (Black was threatening N–KR4).

*16*. ..., N × P!; *17*. N × N, P–QN4; *18*. R–Q4, P–Q4; *19*. P–QN3, N–Q2; *20*. B–N3, B–B3; *21*. R–Q2, N–N3; *22*. R–B1, NP × N; *23*. P × P, Q–B1; *24*. P–B5, N–B5; *25*. R–Q3, (or *25*. B × N, R × P; when Black regains his piece and wins a pawn).

*25*. ..., R–K1; *26*. R–N3, R × P; *27*. R–N8, Q–Q2; *28*. KR–N1, R(B4)–B1; *29*. R × R, R × R; *30*. Q–N3, P–KR4; *31*. P–KR4, P–R4; *32*. P–R4, B–K2; *33*. Q–N7, Q–Q1; *34*. K–N2, B–N5; *35*. Q–N5, a mistake that hastens the end, but in any case he is hopelessly placed.

*35*. ..., N–R6; *36*. R × B, there is nothing to be done against Black's grip on the position.

*36.* ..., N × Q; *37.* R × N, P–B3; *38.* P–B4, R–N1; *39.* R–B5, Q–N3; *40.* R–N5, Q–R2; *41.* R × R ch, and White resigned.

## THE QUEEN'S GAMBIT ACCEPTED

The defences I have shown so far against *1.* P–Q4, are not of course the only defences that come into consideration. There are quite a number which Black can usefully play, and among these the Queen's Gambit Accepted stands out as a solid worthwhile line of strategic value and importance.

| | |
|---|---|
| *1.* P–Q4 | P–Q4 |
| *2.* P–QB4 | P × P |
| *3.* N–KB3 | |

White plays this move first of all (before playing P–K3), since if he tries *3.* P–K3 at once Black livens up matters in his favour with *3.* ..., P–K4.

| | |
|---|---|
| *3.* ... | N–KB3 |

I have already shown that it is bad for Black to cling on to the gambit pawn by *3.* ..., P–QN4; as to which see Chapter 6, page 117.

| | |
|---|---|
| *4.* P–K3 | P–K3 |

Again clinging on to the pawn by *4.* ..., B–K3 leads to positions in White's favour: e.g. *4.* ..., B–K3; *5.* N–B3, B–Q4; *6.* N × B, Q × N; *7.* Q–B2, P–K3; *8.* B × P, B–N5 ch; *9.* K–K2.

| | |
|---|---|
| *5.* B × P | P–B4 |

Having exchanged off a centre pawn for a flank pawn (i.e. having to some extent abandoned control of the centre), Black must attack the White centre with the utmost vigour and as quickly as possible.

| | |
|---|---|
| *6.* O–O | P–QR3 |

Planning to play P–QN4 and then to develop his QB on N2. White at once takes steps to prevent this.

|       |          |        |
|-------|----------|--------|
| 7.    | P–QR4    | N–B3   |
| 8.    | Q–K2     |        |

Not really giving up a pawn, as will soon become apparent.

|       |          |        |
|-------|----------|--------|
| 8.    | ...      | P × P  |
| 9.    | R–Q1     | B–K2   |

Black cannot defend the QP by 9. ..., P–K4; since then 10. P × P, N × P; 11. N × N, would win a piece.

|       |          |        |
|-------|----------|--------|
| 10.   | P × P    | O–O    |
| 11.   | N–B3     | N–Q4   |

Necessary, because White was threatening to play P–Q5. This position is about level. White, with free play for his pieces, can try and attack on the King-side and Black can concentrate his forces on attacking White's isolated pawn on Q4.

124

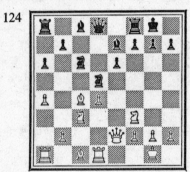

White to play

White now has two possible lines of attack.

*Line 1*

|       |           |             |
|-------|-----------|-------------|
| 12.   | B–Q3      | N(B3)–N5    |
| 13.   | B–N1      | P–QN3       |
| 14.   | P–R5      | P × P       |
| 15.   | N–K4      | B–Q2        |
| 16.   | N–K5      | B–QN4       |

150

With a good game for Black, as in the game Gligoric–Portisch, Bugojno, 1978.

*Line 2* (see Diagram 124)

|  |  |
|---|---|
| *12.* Q–K4 | N–B3 |

Posing a problem for White. Will he accept a draw by repetition of position by *13.* Q–K2, N–Q4; *14.* Q–K4, etc., or will he try for more?

In the game Polugaievsky–Hort, Manila, 1976, he did indeed try for more (and got less). That game continued: *13.* Q–R4, N–Q4; *14.* Q–N4, N–B3; *15.* Q–N3, N–KR4; *16.* Q–R3, N–B3; *17.* B–KN5, N–QN5; *18.* Q–N3, R–K1; *19.* N–K5, N(B3)–Q4; *20.* B–R6, B–B1; *21.* QR–B1, P–QN3; *22.* N × N, P × N; *23.* B–N3, B–K3; *24.* P–R3, R–B1; *25.* R × R, Q × R; *26.* B–KB4, Q–N2; *27.* N–N4, K–R1; *28.* B–Q6, B × N; *29.* P × B, B × B; *30.* Q × B, P–QR4; *31.* R–QB1, P–R3; *32.* R–B7, Q–N1; *33.* Q–Q7 ? ? (a colossal blunder; correct was *33.* P–N3).

*33.* . . ., R–K8 ch; *34.* K–R2, R–QB8; *35.* P–N3, R × R; *36.* Q–Q6, R–N2; White resigns.

## EXERCISES

125

Black to play

1. What should Black play in this position, and why?

126

Black to play

2. Would 6. ..., N–N5 be a good move in this position? If not, why not?

127

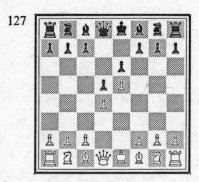

Black to play

3. You are Black in this position in which White has just played 3. P–K5. You can see that White now has more than his fair share of the centre. How are you going to attack the strong position White has built up for himself in the centre? Should you attack it by (a) 3. ..., P–KB3; or by (b) 3. ..., P–QB4 or by (c) 3. ..., N–QB3?

128

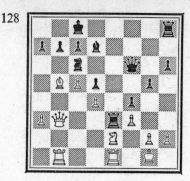

White to play

**4.** Why not play Q × P here?

**5.** After *1.* P–Q4, N–KB3; *2.* P–QB4, P–KN3; what is the point of White playing *3.* P–KN3?

**6.** In the Nimzo-Indian Defence why, after *1.* P–Q4, N–KB3; *2.* P–QB4, P–K3; *3.* N–QB3, does Black play *3.* ..., B–N5?

129

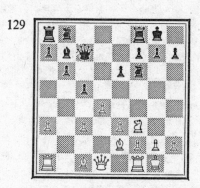

White to play

**7.** In this position, why does White play P–QR4?

8. After *1.* P–Q4, P–Q4; *2.* P–QB4, P × P; why not play *3.* P–K3, and thereby win back the pawn almost at once?

## ANSWERS TO THE EXERCISES

1. (see Diagram 125) Black should play *3.* . . ., P × P; since if he allows White to play *4.* P–Q5, he will lose a lot of space and have a constricted position.

2. (see Diagram 126) *6.* . . ., N–N5 loses a piece after *7.* B–N5 ch, since if then *7.* . . ., B–Q2; *8.* Q × N, or, if *7.* . . ., N–B3; *8.* N × N, P × N; *9.* B × P ch, winning the Rook. So *6.* . . ., N–N5 would be a losing mistake.

3. (see Diagram 127) You should attack White's pawn chain by (*b*) *3.* . . ., P–QB4, since the correct way of dealing with an enemy pawn chain is to attack its base; once that begins to crumble you have practically a won game.

4. (see Diagram 128) If you play Q × P here, Black wins the Queen by B–K3.

5. After *1.* P–Q4, N–KB3; *2.* P–QB4, P–KN3; White plays *3.* P–KN3 because he wants to place his KB on N2, from which point the Bishop can attack the white squares along the long diagonal.

6. Black plays his Bishop to N5 with the primary objective of undermining White's control of his K4, and with the additional notion of exchanging off Bishop for Knight in order to double White's pawns on the QB file and thus render them less mobile.

7. (see Diagram 129) White plays P–QR4 in order to develop his Bishop on R3, thereby pinning a pawn on the Rook.

8. If, after *1.* P–Q4, P–Q4; *2.* P–QB4, P × P; White plays *3.* P–K3, then Black gets a fine game by replying *3.* . . ., P–K4.

# CHAPTER 8

# HINTS ON THE MIDDLE GAME

The middle game is that phase in the game when the players have developed their pieces but have not yet exchanged off most of them to come down to the ending. It is the richest in ideas, since now we get the full orchestration of the game with each and every piece playing its full part in the battle. It also happens to be the least charted and sign-posted of all the phases of the game. Comparatively few books have been written on this aspect of the game, probably because of the difficulty in singling out the most important ideas; and, of those few books, even fewer are good ones.

And yet it is not the most difficult stage in the game for the beginner to master. That invidious distinction is enjoyed by the end game, a phase of the game that is usually mysterious to even the practised and more advanced player. For, whereas the end game may occasionally look like black magic to the ordinary player, the middle game, though not without its mysterious moments, is usually straightforward enough and is dependent on various technical manoeuvres that are easy enough to master.

It may sound prosaic, but there is a curious affinity between the art of the middle game and the art of eating. In both cases you have to be provided with weapons or utensils, and if you use them skilfully enough you will be able to carve up the enemy. In fact, the resemblance goes further and is even to be found in the actual terms employed in both the art of chess and the culinary art: words such as 'fork' and 'skewer' are common to both.

*The Fork*

This is when a piece attacks two or more pieces at the same time, and its strength lies in the fact that the defence cannot remove more than one piece from attack in the one move.

A simple example is to be found in Diagram 130, where the pawn is attacking the King and Queen at the same time, and the Black Queen is lost.

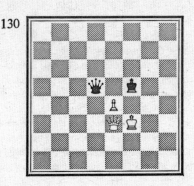

A Knight can do even better, and here is what is known as a family check, for reasons that are fairly obvious. Clearly, the consequences of such a fork are pretty deadly, but I have to

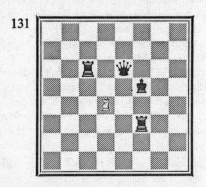

confess that I have been able to administer few family forks in the course of a fairly long chess career. More common and bread-and-butter – as compared to cake – is:

*The Pin*

This is where you are pinning down a piece of lesser value on a piece of greater value so that the smaller-valued piece dare not move or, in cases where the King is concerned, cannot move. The two contrasting examples are to be found in Diagram 132

132

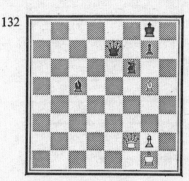

where Black's Knight dare not move for fear of losing the Queen, and White's Queen cannot move because of the indirect attack on the King.

A common example of the pin is to be seen in the following variation of the Ruy Lopez: *1.* P-K4, P-K4; *2.* N-KB3, N-QB3; *3.* B-N5, P-Q3. Known as the Steinitz Defence (after the great Wilhelm Steinitz who was world champion in the last century), this defence is no longer much employed, since it is too passive in the way it voluntarily submits to a pin of the Knight.

This shows how useful the pin can be and, if it is useful by itself, it becomes doubly useful when united with the fork. A modern example occurred in a game, J. Seirawan–M. Videnkeller in the Junior World Championship at Skien in Norway, 1979 (Diagram 133). Here White won by *1.* R × P, when if the Rook sacrifice is accepted we get the following sequence of fork and pin: *1.* ..., K × R; *2.* N-N5 ch, P × N (or *2.* ..., K-N1 or R1; *3.* N × B, with a fork by the Knight on the enemy Queen and

Rook); *3*. Q–R5 ch, and (the pawn being pinned on the King by the White Bishop) Black must play *3*. ..., K–N1 or N2; after which he is mated by *4*. Q × P ch, K–R1; *5*. Q–R7 mate.

133

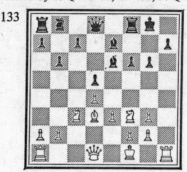

White to play

Seeing all this, Black in fact played *1*. ..., P–KB4; and still lost eventually.

*The Skewer*

This might be regarded as a pin placed upside down, and consists of an attack on an enemy piece in line with another enemy piece so that these pieces appear to be speared on a skewer. One enemy

134

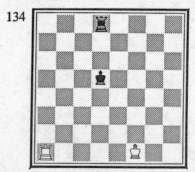

White to play

piece has to move away from the attack, and then you capture the other as in Diagram 134. White plays *1.* R–Q1 ch, and the Black King moves out of check, allowing White to capture the Rook with *2.* R × R.

*Discovered Check*

This is a very powerful weapon and usually results in complete destruction of the opponent. It is not a straightforward check, but is a check delivered by moving one piece and uncovering a check from another piece.

White to play

In Diagram 135, White's King is already in check and Black seems to be winning comfortably. But suddenly White discovers check with *1.* N–B6, and it is Black who is quite lost.

Another even more potent form of discovered check is:

*Double Check*

This occurs when you give check with the piece that does the discovery, as in Diagram 136. Though White is materially down (he has a Rook for the enemy Queen) he can now force mate in two moves by a double check: *1.* N–B6 double check, K–R1; *2.* R–N8 mate.

White to play

## Smothered Mate

This is a mate which often arises out of discovered and double checks. The mate is an astonishing affair in which the hapless King is smothered to death by its own pieces, an extreme example being in Diagram 137. In this position, with White to play, he

White to play

delivers mate by *1*. N–B7. Far-fetched and unlikely, you might think. How is such an extraordinary mate to be accomplished? Well, one way of accomplishing it is by:

160

*Philidor's Legacy*

Named after the great French master and musician, André Danican Philidor, this is achieved in most elegant and pleasing style.

Look at the position in Diagram 138 which occurred in a game,

138

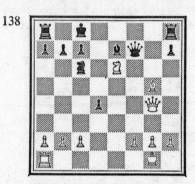

White to play

Paul Morphy–F. Schrufer, Paris, 1859. White played *1.* N–B5 dis ch, K–N1; forced since *1.* ..., K–Q1; *2.* Q–Q7 is mate.

*2.* N–Q7 ch, K–B1; *3.* N–N6 db. ch, K–N1; *4.* Q–B8 ch, R × Q; *5.* N–Q7 mate.

*Unpinning*

Just as there are known and typical ways of pinning the opponent, so there are such ways to unpin one's own forces. When you are suffering from some troublesome pin, your first thought should be to look around and see if you can relieve this pin, that is to say, escape from it, by a check. Diagram 139 will show a typical and brilliant example of this unpinning process. It is from a game, A. Tchernin–P. Nikolic, Junior World Championship at Skien, Norway, 1979.

White relieved the pin on his Knight by *1.* R × N ch, K × R; *2.* N × R. Now he has won a piece, *but* there comes a fresh and

161

even more dangerous pin with *2. ...,* Q–B8 ch; *3.* B–B1, B–R6; when not only does Black threaten to get his piece back but he also menaces White with mate. Again relief comes through

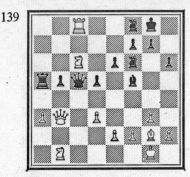

139

White to play

a check. *4.* Q–N4 ch, K–N1; *5.* N–Q2, Q–K8; yet again a pin but *6.* Q–N1, Q × N; *7.* N–N3, Q–N4; *8.* B × B, Q–R4; *9.* B–B1, resigns.

## The Dangerous Bishop

Beginners always imagine that the mysterious Knight, with its lopsided move, is the really dangerous minor piece. They are quite wrong in this. It is in fact the long-ranging Bishop that can do the most damage once it runs riot along the diagonal.

In fact, the motto *Beware the KB on the long diagonal* should always be borne in mind. If White had done so in the position shown in Diagram 140 he would never have so wantonly opened up the dangerous long diagonal, though admittedly the idea by which he did so was a tempting one.

The position shown in Diagram 140 occurred in a game played at Tashkent in 1979 between O. Korneshov and A. Tashkhodyaev; and White now played *1.* P–QN4?, N × NP; *2.* Q–R4 ch, N–B3; *3.* P–Q5, winning the Knight but opening up the long diagonal (QR1–KR8).

*3.* ..., N–Q2!; *4.* P × N, B × N ch; *5.* B–Q2, B × R; the Black Bishop now reigns supreme along the long diagonal and White is curiously helpless against this.

140

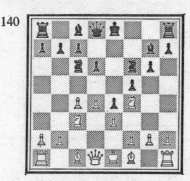

White to play

*6.* N–K6, N–N3; and White resigned because of *7.* P × P dis ch, N × Q; *8.* N × Q (if *8.* P × R = Q, simply B × N wins for Black).

*8.* ..., B × P; *9.* N × B, R–QN1; *10.* N–R5, R–N8 ch; *11.* K–K2, N–B6 ch; *12.* B × N, B × B; and once again this Bishop is all-powerful, and White has to allow it to capture the Knight for fear of being mated.

## Two Bishops

If one Bishop can be dangerous, then two have the strength of ten, and you would be well advised to try and secure the advantage of two Bishops by exchanging off a Knight for a Bishop in most circumstances of the game.

In Diagram 141 White has two fine Bishops that are raking Black's King-side, whereas Black's Knight and Bishop are comparatively impotent. In addition, White's Queen is centralized as opposed to the decentralized Black Queen, and it is little wonder that White forced the win by a series of delightful pins. This was in a game J. Seirawan–G. Barbero, Junior World Championship at Skien in Norway, 1979.

141

White to play

White won by *1.* R × P ch, K × R; or *1.* ..., K–R1; *2.* Q–KN5, P × Q; *3.* R × NP dis ch and mates in two moves (the first pin).

*2.* Q–N5 ch (the second pin), K–B2; if *2.* ..., K–R1; *3.* Q–R6 ch, K–N1; Q–R7 mate.

*3.* Q × BP ch, K–K1; *4.* B–N6 ch, N–B2; *5.* B–K5 (the third pin), resigns.

He cannot play *5.* ..., Q × B; because of *6.* Q × Q ch (the fourth pin). So he must move his Queen, say to N7, and then comes simply *6.* B × BP, with mate on Q8 – the best pin of all!

*Power of the Passed Pawn*

Whilst the passed pawn usually makes its strength felt in the ending, there are quite a number of occasions during the middle game when its force becomes apparent.

Diagram 142 is from a game, P. Dontschev–P. Hegse, played at Warna, 1979. Black's passed King's pawn at once makes its strength known by *1.* ..., P–K6; *2.* R–K2, N × P; and White resigned because of *3.* R × N, R–Q8 ch; *4.* R × R, Q × R ch; *5.* K–R2, R × R ch; *6.* B × R, P–K7; and the pawn cannot be prevented from Queening.

142

Black to play

## Co-operation of the Pieces

In the middle game – as indeed in every phase of the game, but it comes out most strongly in the middle game – it is of vital importance that you should learn how the pieces work together. Unless they co-operate to the full you will find that your plans fail for want of joint power and you will be like the commander of an army which is in a constant state of confusion and disorder.

We have already seen how two Bishops can work together to perfection, but the same also applies to an assortment of pieces. A Queen and Rook or Rooks can be devastating along a file or a rank. A Queen and Bishop can form a mating net by occupying

143

diagonals around the enemy King; a Queen and Knight can constitute a mating attack by an onslaught on the enemy's KB2 or KR2 if he has castled; even a Queen and a pawn can form an irresistible mating combination as, for example, in Diagram 143. This is a simple but constantly recurring group of pieces.

For something more complicated but equally characteristic, look at Diagram 144. If it were Black to play here, he could use

144

his Queen and Knight in co-operation to force a win by N × B ch. But if it is White's move, then the co-operation between the pieces becomes enormous and includes every single piece on the board. Play would proceed *1.* R–R7 ch, K × R; if *1. . . .,* K–N1; *2.* Q × P mate – perfect co-operation between Queen and Rook.

*2.* Q × P ch, and if now *2. . . .,* K–R3; *3.* Q × P mate (co-operation of Queen and Bishop).

So *2. . . .,* K–R1; *3.* R–R1 ch, Q–R4; *4.* R × Q ch, P × R; *5.* Q–R7 mate. Right to the end, White's pieces are co-operating while Black's QR stands idly by, a silent and useless spectator.

Co-operation between pieces can be so great that a player can afford to give up his Queen in order to maintain or increase this co-operation. For an example of this look at Diagram 145. This is a variation from a game, Golombek–H. E. Price, Hastings, 1932/3, for which White was awarded a brilliancy prize. White

now plays *1.* N × B, and after *1.* ..., Q × Q; *2.* B × P mate.
The perfect co-operation between Bishop and Knight has enabled
White to dispense entirely with his Queen.

145

White to play

## Power of the Sacrifice

You will have noticed running through this whole chapter the
theme of the power of mind over matter, which is a basic theme,
and even a *raison d'être*, of the game of chess. Books have been
written on typical sacrifices and I can only hope here to give a
sample of the riches of sacrificial combinations in which chess
rejoices.

One very commonly recurring theme is the sacrifice of the
Bishop for the RP in order to force a mating attack. Removal
of the KRP so weakens the defences of the enemy King that it
cannot withstand a determined onslaught. Consider the position
in Diagram 146, where the White pieces stand ready to assault
the King-side.

This position arose in a game, I. Yunkhin–Sh. Lyulinsky at
Tashkent, 1979. Now came a break-through on the KR file by
*1.* B × P ch, K × B; *2.* Q–R5 ch, K–N1; *3.* N–B5, Q–B4;
*4.* R–KR3, P–B3; *5.* Q–R7 ch, K–B2; *6.* Q × P ch, K–K1;
*7.* R–R7, B–B3; *8.* N × P, this Knight cannot be taken because

167

146

White to play

of mate on K7; it was however important to remove the QP so as to open up a further line of attack (the Q file) on the enemy King.

8. ..., N–K4; 9. N × B, N–B2; if 9. ..., N × N; 10. Q–Q7, mate and if 9. ..., Q × N; 10. Q–K7, mate. 10. Q × P, Q × N; 11. R–K1, resigns. After 11. ..., K–Q2; 12. R × N ch, R × R; 13. Q × R ch, K–Q1; 14. R × P, Q–Q2; 15. Q–B6 ch, K–B1; (or K–B2; 16. R–K7, winning the Queen).

16. R–Q6, Q–QB2; 17. R–B6, winning the Queen.

147

White to play

This was essentially an eliminatory sacrifice. There are many such sacrifices, and another of even more violent character can be seen in Diagram 147. This came in a game, Fuller–Bachtiar, Australia, 1975. It is clear that the key to Black's defences lies in his Rook on Q1. Once this is eliminated, his resistance is at an end. Play went *1.* Q × R ch, K × Q; *2.* R–R8 ch, N–B1; *3.* R(R8) × N ch, Q–K1; *4.* R × Q mate.

## Comparative Value of the Pieces

It is essential to have some means, however rough and approximate, of judging the relative value of the pieces. Unless you have this, you cannot know when it is right to exchange off pieces or to refuse and avoid the exchange. Nor can you plan the gain of material or make an attack on the opponent with a view to winning material.

Taking as a basic unit the weakest chess-piece – the pawn – it is usual to regard three of these as being worth a minor piece: a Knight or a Bishop. A Knight and a Bishop are roughly equal, the Knight being better at the beginning and the Bishop better at the closing stages of the game when there are wide areas in which the Bishop can comfortably move.

A Rook is worth a minor piece plus two pawns. Two minor pieces are worth a Rook and two pawns, the exception to this being two Bishops, which are worth more than this.

The Queen is about the equivalent of two Rooks, and three minor pieces are worth more than a Queen.

## EXERCISES

148

Black to play

1. What happens if Black plays 5. . . ., QN–Q2 here?

149

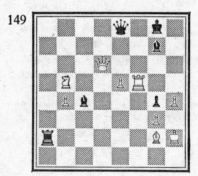

Black to play

2. How does Black administer the *coup de grâce*?

150

White to play

3. What should happen if White plays Q × KP?

151

Black to play

4. Why would *1.* ..., K–Q4 now be a deadly mistake?

152

White to play

**5.** Technically, White is material down. If Black gets going, then White will lose; moreover, White is in check – how does he fend it off?

153

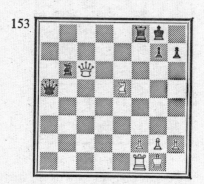

White to play

**6.** White to play and win – how?

154

White to play

**7.** Why is it wrong to play P–QN4 here?

155

White to play

**8.** White to play and win – how?

156

Black to play

**9.** How can Black take advantage of the fact that White's King-side pawns have become seriously weakened (there is a *hole* where a Bishop should be)?

157

White to play

**10.** Again a hole and the possibility of eliminating the Bishop that guards this hole – how is this done, and what effect does it have?

## ANSWERS TO THE EXERCISES

1. (see Diagram 148) White mates Black by 6. ..., N–Q6 here.

2. (see Diagram 149) Black wins by 1. ..., Q–R1.

3. (see Diagram 150) After 1. Q × KP, there comes 1. ..., Q–R8 ch; 2. K–R2, B–Q4 ch; forking King and Queen.

4. (see Diagram 151) Because of the skewer by 2. Q–B3 ch, winning the Queen.

5 (see Diagram 152) He fends off the check by a discovered check: 1. N–K5 dis ch, K–R1 (if 1. ..., K–B1; 2. Q–B7 mate); 2. Q–R6 ch, K–N1; 3. Q–R7 ch, K–B1; 4. Q–B7 mate.

6. (see Diagram 153) White wins by 1. Q–K6 ch, K–R1; 2. N–B7 ch, K–N1; if 2. ..., R × N; 3. Q–K8 ch, followed by mate. 3. N–R6 db ch, K–R1; 4. Q–N8 ch, R × Q; 5. N–B7 mate.

7. (see Diagram 154) It is wrong to play P–QN4 here because of the reply N × KP; 2. P × N, B × R.

8. (see Diagram 155) White wins by 1. B × P ch, K × B; 2. N–N5 ch, and now there are four possible King moves: (a) 2. ..., K–R1; 3. Q–R5 ch, K–N1; 4. Q–R7 mate. (b) 2. ..., K–N1; 3. Q–R5, and Black can only avoid mate by giving up his Queen for the Knight. (c) 2. ..., K–R3; 3. N × KP discovered check followed by N × Q. (d) 2. ..., K–N3; 3. Q–Q3 ch, P–B4 (3. ..., K–R4; 4. Q–R7 ch, K–N5; 5. Q–R3 mate). 4. P × P e.p. ch, K × P; 5. R × P mate.

9. (see Diagram 156) This came from a game, I. Ramanie–O. Koloyartseva, Vitebsk, 1979. Black won by 1. R × P; 2. K × R, Q–R7 ch; and White resigns because of 3. K–B1, R–B1 ch, with mate to follow.

10. (see Diagram 157) White must eliminate the KB which can protect the hole. This was from a game played at Decin, 1979, between J. Reznicek and W. Heimig. White won by *1*. R × B ch, K × R; *2*. B–R6 ch, K–N1; *3*. N–Q5, N–Q6 dis ch; *4*. N × Q, N × Q; *5*. N–K7 ch, K–R1; *6*. N × R, B–K3; *7*. N–B7, P–B6; *8*. N × B, resigns. (If *8*. . . ., P × P; *9*. B–N7 mate.)

# CHAPTER 9

# HINTS ON THE END GAME

It is in the end game that the King comes into his own. Since it cannot be captured, the one great danger that may prevent its use as a fighting piece lies in the ultimate sanction of checkmate. But, in the ending, so many pieces, major and minor, have been exchanged that neither side really disposes of sufficient fighting material to make checkmate a likely consummation. Or, if there is sufficient, it is only barely so; the fact that usually both sides possess this bare sufficiency means that this balance cancels out the danger of the King succumbing to checkmate by venturing into the fray.

Since the King is so powerful in the ending, you get the first general principle which is vitally important and must always be borne in mind: bring the King on the scene of action with the utmost speed. I have seen so many games lost through the neglect of this golden rule that I must emphasize: you should almost instinctively move your King to wherever the centre of the action is, just as soon as you get down to the end game.

In fact, all the hints I shall give you on the endings involve the use of the King; when I mention some of the hints under the name of the piece or pieces which are employed in that particular part of my advice, it should be taken for granted that the King will be the main collaborator with the piece or pieces in question.

## THE OPPOSITION

The theme of my introduction to this chapter becomes most clear in the matter of the Opposition, by which is meant the opposition of King against King. Since, by the rules of the game, the Kings cannot come into contact with each other, it follows that there must be at least one square in between them. Hence, when the Kings are so placed opposite each other by a bare minimum of one square a state of opposition occurs, in the technical sense that I have employed here. This opposition can be vertical as in Diagram 158, or horizontal as in Diagram 159, or diagonal as in

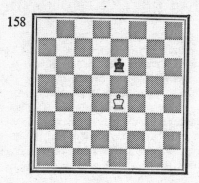

158

Diagram 160. Whatever type of opposition it may be, there exists a sort of frontier line running between the Kings across which the King of the player whose turn it is to move cannot pass.

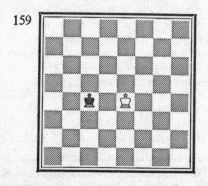

159

Since he cannot go forward he must give way, either by moving back or sideways. Thus, in Diagram 158, if it is White's turn to move, his King cannot go forward to K5, Q5 or KB5, but must either retreat backwards to the third rank or move sideways to either KB4 or Q4.

If you analyse all these moves, you will find that White gives ground in every case. If he moves to K3, Q3 or B3, then the Black

160

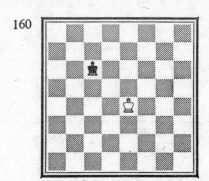

King can come up to the fourth rank; equally, if the White King moves sideways, the Black King can gain the fourth rank by making a diagonal step forward to either KB4 or Q4, according to which way the White King goes.

This then is a method of beating back the King without directly attacking it; and when we say that one side or the other has the opposition, we mean that he is in a position to force back the enemy King by this process.

This gives us the rule that, in such circumstances, the side whose turn it is *not* to move has the opposition.

If you turn back to Chapter 5 you will find that this use of the opposition can be one of the main steps in reducing the space enjoyed by the opposing King, and is a necessary adjunct to mating with King and Rook or with King and two Bishops. But where the opposition is of the utmost importance is in King and pawn endings when, quite often, the fact that one has or has not the opposition may make the difference between a win and a loss, or between a win and a draw.

## KING AND PAWN ENDINGS

The simplest type of King and pawn ending is when one side (White in this case) has been left with one pawn and the other with none; in order to win, White will have to force his pawn through to become promoted to a Queen. Once this is achieved, he can force checkmate as given in Chapter 2, page 43.

Consider, however, the position given in Diagram 161. With

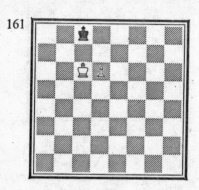

161

White to move, it is Black who has the opposition, so there is no question of White's King being able to advance. Nor is there any point in his retreating with his King or in his moving sideways. So, in order to advance, he must play *1.* P–Q7 ch, and Black must then play K–Q1 if he wants to prevent the pawn from queening.

What is White to do next? Any move away from the pawn allows Black to capture it, so he must play *2.* K–Q6 and the game is a draw by stalemate.

Now go back to Diagram 161 and suppose it is not White's turn to move but Black's, that is to say, suppose that White has the opposition. Then Black has to play *1.* ..., K–Q1; as K–N1 allows White to play P–Q7, followed next move by P–Q8 = Q ch.

White replies *2.* P–Q7 and Black has only one move *2.* ...,

K–K2; whereupon White replies *3.* K–B7, queening his pawn next move.

Push the White King one square back and bring the Black King one square forward (as in Diagram 162) and you find that,

162

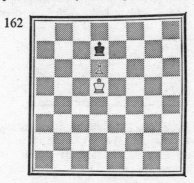

White to play

no matter whose turn it is to move, White must sooner or later lose the opposition and the ending will be drawn. For example, with White to play, there comes *1.* K–K5, K–Q1; *2.* K–K6, K–K1; and now Black has the opposition and White has nothing better than *3.* P–Q7 ch, K–Q1; *4.* K–Q6, stalemate. It makes no difference if, on move *1*, White plays K–B5, as then comes *1.* ..., K–Q1; *2.* K–B6, K–B1; *3.* P–Q7 ch, K–Q1; *4.* K–Q6, stalemate.

Now, however, reverse the position of White King and pawn, and White can force a win, no matter whose turn it is to move (as in Diagram 163). With Black to play, White wins simply after *1.* ..., K–B1; *2.* K–K7, followed by the advance of the pawn to queen. Or if *1.* ..., K–K1; *2.* K–B7 and again the pawn must queen.

With White to play, he has to make use of his pawn move to secure the opposition. *1.* K–B6, K–B1 (or *1.* ..., K–K1; *2.* K–B7, and the pawn advances to Queen).

*2.* P–Q6, K–Q1; *3.* P–Q7, K–K2; *4.* K–B7, etc.

163

So the moral is: as long as White has the opposition and can maintain that opposition, he is able to win such pawn endings.

Push the White pawn right back to its second rank and you can still win with the opposition. Here, with Black to play, he

164

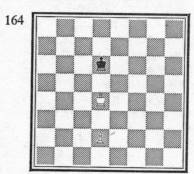

Black to play

must give way with his King by *1.* ..., K–B3; *2.* K–K5, K–B4; or *2.* ..., K–Q2; *3.* K–Q5, and, by the use of opposition, the enemy King is beaten back still further.

*3.* P–Q4 ch, K–B3; *4.* K–K6, K–B2; *5.* P–Q5, K–Q1; *6.* K–Q6, and we have the position as in Diagram 163, when White wins easily enough.

It should be noted that this kind of win applies to all pawns, with the one exception of the Rook pawn which poses special difficulties, since it is impossible to force the enemy King out of the corner. No matter whose turn it is to move in Diagram 165,

165

the ending is drawn. If it is White, then *1*. K–N4, K–N3; *2*. P–R4, K–R3; *3*. P–R5, K–R2; *4*. K–N5, K–N2; *5*. P–R6 ch, K–R2; *6*. K–R5, K–R1; *7*. K–N6, K–N1; *8*. P–R7 ch, K–R1; *9*. K–R6, stalemate.

Pawn promotions are among the most colourful paradoxes in chess, and there are many situations in which they will bring a sudden change in fortunes.

166

Black to play

In Diagram 166, with Black to play, he has a comfortable draw by *1. ...,* R-Q1; *2.* R-KN1, R-KN1; followed by bringing the Black King over to KB3 and winning the pawn. But supposing he is greedy and careless, he may play *1. ...,* R-N4; directly attacking the pawn, and then comes *2.* R-K5 ch, R × R; *3.* P-N8 = Q, and White wins.

167

White to play

Just as nasty a shock would afflict Black in the position in Diagram 167 where, in order to be doubly safe, he has both his pieces fixed on the queening square of the White QRP. But now comes *1.* Q × N, Q × Q; *2.* P-R8 = Q ch, and Black is quite lost.

## ROOK AND PAWN ENDINGS

These are common and, alas, very difficult. But there are certain basic principles that apply to all Rook and pawn endings, a knowledge of which will help you in dealing with what is commonly mishandled. One principle is always to try and keep your Rook in as active a position as possible. By active I really mean attacking, for the side that keeps his Rook in a passive (i.e. defensive) position is at a grave disadvantage. Another rule to bear in mind is: if you wish to keep a hold and a check on enemy passed pawns, place your Rook behind them rather than in front, since then they are much more active.

184

An example of the possibilities of such an ending and an illustration of how easy it is to go wrong in a Rook and pawn ending can be seen in Diagram 168 which is a position that arose in a game, Korchnoi–Miles at Kapstadt in South Africa, 1979.

168

Black to play

In this position Black is actually a pawn up, but he has two disadvantages (a backward and weak pawn on KB2 and a passive and vulnerable King); whereas White has a most dangerous passed pawn. Adding these factors up, it has to be admitted that Black will have to be careful to secure the draw.

He played *33. ..., K–B2?*, obviously trying to deal with the passed pawn. Instead, he should have placed his Rook behind the enemy pawn with *33. ..., R–QN6*.

White seized his opportunity with *34. R–B6, R–KR6*. Exchange of Rooks leads to a loss after *34. ..., R × R; 35. P × R, P–N4; 36. P × P, P–R5; 37. P–N6, P–R6; 38. P × P, P–R7; 39. P–B8 = Q, P–R8 = Q; 40. K × P, Q–K8 ch; 41. K–B5, Q–B8 ch; 42. K–N6, Q–N7 ch; 43. K–R7, Q–K5 ch; 44. K–N8*, and White escapes from the checks to win, since if *44. ..., Q–N5 ch; 45. Q–N7 ch*, or if *44. ..., Q–Q4 ch; 45. Q–B7 ch.*

*35. R × P ch, K–N3; 36. R–B6 ch, K × P; 37. R × P, R × P; 38. K × P, K–B4; 39. R–KR6, R–KN5; 40. K–B5, K–Q4;*

*41.* P–N6, R–N8; *42.* K–B6, R–B8 ch; *43.* K–K7, R–K8 ch; *44.* K–B7, R–B8 ch; *45.* K–N8, and Black resigns. He can only stop the NP from queening by giving up his Rook for the pawn.

## KNIGHT VERSUS BISHOP IN THE ENDING

The contrast between the action of the Bishop and that of the Knight is most marked in the ending. The Bishop is better in open spaces when it can sweep down the diagonals, but it is worse in close positions where it is impeded by fixed pawn chains. Normally the numerous exchanges that have taken place before the ending is reached tend to favour the Bishop, but there are occasions on which the pawn chains still exist and when these interfere badly with the action of the Bishop.

Such an occasion is to be seen in Diagram 169 where nearly all the Black pawns are on black squares and greatly impede the action of the Bishop. This position arose in a game, Lenk–Genov, played in a team match in East Germany, 1979.

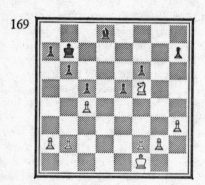

169

White to play

First of all, the players brought their pieces to the scene of the action: *27.* K–K2, K–B3; *28.* K–Q3, K–Q2; *29.* K–K4, K–K3; *30.* P–KN4, B–B2; *31.* P–KR4, B–Q1; *32.* P–R5, P–QR3; *33.* P–R4, putting an end to Black's attempts to break open the diagonal for his Bishop, which remains bottled in till the end of the game.

33. ..., B–B2; *34.* P–B3, B–Q1; *35.* P–R6, B–B2; *36.* N–N7 ch, K–Q2; *37.* K–B5, K–B3; *38.* N–K6, B–Q3; *39.* K × P, P–N4; *40.* RP × P ch, P × P; *41.* P–N3, P × P; *42.* P × P, resigns. White simply advances his NP and eventually promotes a pawn to Queen.

## ZUGZWANG

This curious-looking German word, which means compulsion to move, is a phenomenon more often seen in draughts than in chess. But it does occur in chess, particularly in the ending, and it describes a situation where a player has to make a move that is to his disadvantage. In short, it is a position where no good move exists.

A good example is to be found in the only chess problem composed by the great American player, Paul Morphy, well over a century ago. It is a simple problem and was composed by the

170

White to play and mate in
two moves

great Morphy when he was still a boy. White mates in two, starting with *1.* R–R6, and Black is in zugzwang. If he moves the Bishop he is mated by R × P and if he takes the Rook by *1.* ..., P × R; then P–N7 is mate.

## EXERCISES

171

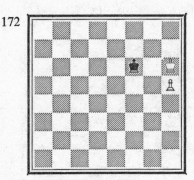

1. In this position, with Black to play, who has the opposition?

172

White to play

2. Can White win? If so, how?

173

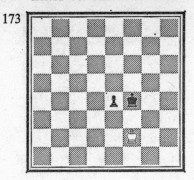

3. Black to play – can he win?

174

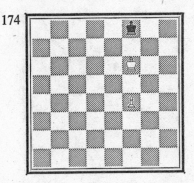

4. White to play. Can he win? If so, how?

175

5. Black to play – how does he win material now?

176

6. White to play and mate in two moves.

177

7. White to play – can he win?

178

8. Black to play – how should the game go?

## ANSWERS TO THE EXERCISES

1. (see Diagram 171) White has the opposition since, after *1.*
..., P–R3; *2.* P–R3, P–R4; *3.* P–R4, Black is forced to move
his King. Or Black may play *1.* ..., P–R4; to which White
replies *2.* P–R4, and again White has the opposition.

2. (see Diagram 172) No. White cannot win since, after *1.* K–R7,
K–B2; *2.* P–R6, K–B1; White has the choice between *3.* K–R8,
K–B2; *4.* P–R7, K–B1; stalemate and *3.* K–N6, K–N1; *4.*
P–R7 ch, K–R1; *5.* K–R6, stalemate.

3. (see Diagram 173) No, because of *1.* ..., P–K6 ch; *2.* K–K2,
K–K5 ; *3.* K–K1, K–Q6; *4.* K–Q1, P–K7 ch; *5.* K–K1,
K–K6 stalemate.

4. (see Diagram 174) Yes, he wins by *1.* P–B5, and if (*a*) *1.* ...,
K–N1; *2.* K–K7. K–N2; *3.* P–B6 ch, and the pawn queens. Or
(*b*) *1.* ..., K–K1; *2.* K–N7, and he brings the pawn down as in
the first variation.

5. (see Diagram 175) Black forces the win of material by *1.*
..., Q × N; *2.* Q × Q, P–R8 = Q ch; and, with a full Bishop
more, has an easy win.

6. (see Diagram 176) White mated in two, starting off with *1.*
N–Q6, and not by *1.* N × N, which is stalemate.

7. (see Diagram 177) No, he cannot win because of *1.* P–B8 = Q,
P–N8 = N ch; *2.* K–R2, N–B6 ch; with a draw by perpetual
check, since White cannot play *3.* K–R1, on account of *3.*
..., R–N8 mate; and must submit to the draw by *3.* K–R3,
N–N8; etc.

8. (see Diagram 178) Black wins by *1.* ..., B–R5; *2.* N–R1,
K–B5; *3.* K–Q1, K–B6; *4.* K–B1, P–B5; *5.* K–Q1, K–N7; *6.*
K–Q2, P–B6 ch; *7.* K–Q3, B–K8; *8.* K–K2, K × P; *9.* K × B,
K–N8; *10.* N–B2, P–B7; and one of the two pawns becomes a
Queen.

# CHAPTER 10

# THE RULES

So much of the spirit of the game is embodied in the rules that it is important to have a firm grasp of them and to obey them practically without having to think about them, if you wish to enjoy playing chess. In the course of a long career playing chess I have found that those players who do not have a clear understanding of the rules are just as muzzy in their comprehension of the game. By the same token, those who spend most of their time at the chess-board in a futile attempt at cutting corners in the rules actually leave themselves with insufficient time and energy to play the game successfully.

Perhaps no section of the rules has been so misused and misunderstood as the 'touch-piece move' rule. Yet the rule is quite clear here and one would have thought left no margin for error or lack of comprehension. Perhaps here a subconscious desire to retrace one's steps and change one's mind after having committed a mistake is responsible. If so, remember what the ancient Greek playwright wrote: 'Over the past the Gods themselves have no power', and allow your move to rest without repining over its inadequacy.

To recap: if you touch one of your own pieces you must move it, if it is legally possible. If it is not legally possible, there is no penalty and you are allowed to move any other piece you like.

If you touch one of the enemy pieces, then you must capture it if this is legally possible, and again there is no penalty if this is not legally possible.

If you fail to execute the move (that is to say, if your fingers have not left the piece when you move it to another square) you are allowed to prolong its journey and play it to another square or, for that matter, shorten its journey. The whole point depends on whether your fingers have quitted the piece or not.

There always seems to be some confusion as to how the touch-piece move affects castling, probably because this is a composite move, a joint move of King and Rook. In castling, you should first get hold of the King and then the Rook, executing the manoeuvre if it is legally possible. If it is not legally possible you must move the King, providing there is a legal move of the King, otherwise there is no penalty.

Whilst on the subject of castling, let me recap the rules: you cannot castle out of or into check. You cannot castle over a check (that is to say, you cannot castle with the King across a square threatened or indeed occupied by the enemy). I use the words 'with the King' advisedly, since the Rook may, if it likes, move across a square threatened by the enemy. This arises only in cases of Queen-side castling, as in Diagram 179. Here White

179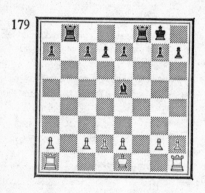

cannot castle King-side since the KB file (across which the King has to travel) is attacked and governed by the enemy Rook. He can, however, castle Queen-side, even though the Rook has to pass over a square attacked by the enemy, since the King is not concerned in the threat. Similarly, whilst the King cannot castle out of check, there is no reason why the Rook should not castle out of attack. In Diagram 179 White may castle Queen-side even though in so doing he moves his QR out of attack.

Finally, I should repeat that you cannot castle at all if your King has already moved, and you may not castle with a Rook that has already been moved. And remember this applies even if the piece has been returned to its original square by yet another move.

Another section of the rules which is a little obscure is that applying to the draw, in particular the draw by repetition of position. Here the rule is that the game is drawn 'upon a claim by one of the players when the same position (*a*) is about to appear or (*b*) has appeared for the third time, the same player having the move each time'. I think it is this last proviso that makes the rule somewhat mystifying. But it is important to bear in mind that it must be the same player on the move each time.

There is another interesting rule relating to the draw which is meant to avoid the tedium of having to play an inordinate number of moves in a manifestly drawn position. This is the fifty-move rule, which states that a game is drawn when a player having the move can show that at least fifty consecutive moves have been made by each side without the capture of any piece or the movement of any pawn. This is a comparatively rare occurrence; but it does occur and I can remember claiming and obtaining a draw under this rule once in my chess career – against the Belgian grandmaster O'Kelly de Galway at a big international tournament in Belgrade, 1952.

When you reach the stage of playing in club matches or tournaments, you will find there are quite a number of rules relating to the use of the chess-clock; but by that time no doubt you will have acquired a book giving the official rules.

## EXERCISES

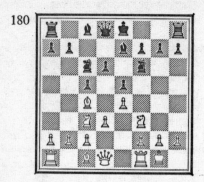

180

1. What should happen if White plays here N–Q5, puts the Knight back on QB3 and moves his Queen to K2 instead?

2. What should happen if, in the position given in Diagram 180, Black plays B–K3 and then, without letting go of the Bishop, moves it on to N5?

3. If, again in Diagram 180, White takes hold of the enemy pawn on KB7, and then puts it back and plays B–K3, what should happen?

4. If the Black pawn on KB7 in Diagram 180 has been somewhat misplaced and is partially on KB8 and partially on KB7 and White adjusts it on KB7 saying '*j'adoube*' or 'I adjust' or some such phrase, need he play B × P ch in accordance with the touch-piece move rule?

181

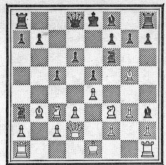

5. If White tries to castle King-side here, what should happen?

6. If, in Diagram 181, White tries to castle Queen-side, what should happen?

7. If, in Diagram 181, White tries to castle Queen-side by first touching his Rook and then his King in making the move, what should happen?

### ANSWERS TO THE EXERCISES

1. (see Diagram 180) He must put the Q back on Q1 and play N–Q5.

2. (see Diagram 180) Nothing should happen; providing Black's fingers have not quitted the piece, the prolonged move is quite legal.

3. (see Diagram 180) White must return his Bishop to QB1 and play B × P ch.

4. (see Diagram 180) No, he need not play B × P ch, always providing he remembers to warn his opponent that he is making an adjustment.

5. (see Diagram 181) Since he cannot castle King-side owing to the presence of the enemy Bishop on Black's KR6, he must replace the KR and move his King elsewhere.

6. (see Diagram 181) Nothing should happen. White is perfectly entitled to castle Queen-side, even though the enemy Knight is attacking a square across which the Rook must move.

7. (see Diagram 181) The controller of the event in which the players are playing, or, if there is no controller, the player's opponent, should tell him he must touch his King first when castling; but there is no penalty.

# CHAPTER 11

# ILLUSTRATIVE GAMES

The following games, which were all played in modern tournaments, have been chosen partly because of their interest and beauty and partly because of their instructional value, in that they show how the mind of a good chess-player works. For this latter purpose I have annotated the moves as fully as possible, but have not tried to be exhaustive, since if I mention and examine every possible variation you would not see the wood for the trees.

In fact, the mind of all chess-players, no matter how strong or how weak they may be, works in a selective fashion. You have to pick out what is essential and meaningful and, in the process, discard the trifling and the unimportant. So I have ignored the lines of play that I regard as insignificant and have left it to the reader's good sense to work out what would happen in cases that I deem of trifling importance.

The reader should play through these games at least twice. On the first occasion you should look more at the game than at my notes, so as to enable yourself to form a general picture of the progress of the game. On the second time of playing, however, it is the notes rather than the actual game on which attention should be concentrated. Remember: these games were not played casually or quickly by their players, so do the games justice by treating them with the same serious care that the actual players gave to them.

## GAME 1

This was played in the 30th Women's Championship of the R.S.F.S.R. (the Federated Russian Soviet Republic) at Kaluga in the U.S.S.R. in 1979.

WHITE: L. SAOONINA          BLACK: I. ABROSHINA
(French Defence)

### *1.* P–K4                                P–K3

The French Defence, one of the most popular defences to White's
*1.* P–K4, and a defence that has proved its worth over the
centuries. The idea is to build up a solid pawn centre and at the
same time to counter-attack against White's own centre. Its chief
virtue is that it is a fighting defence; as for its disadvantages, well,
see how this game goes. Also see Chapter 7, page 134.

### *2.* P–Q4                                P–Q4

Both sides continue to occupy the centre, and now White is faced
with the problem: what to do with the threatened KP. Basically,
she has three possible ways of solving the problem: to protect the
pawn with the Knight by either N–QB3 or N–Q2; to exchange
off pawns by *3.* P × P; or to advance the pawn by *3.* P–K5. As
to the relative merits of these moves, see Chapter 7, page 135.

### *3.* N–Q2

A method of play that has become increasingly popular in the
last twenty years. Whilst not perhaps quite so attacking as
N–QB3, it has the advantage of preventing Black from continuing his counter-attack by B–N5 which would now be met by
*4.* P–QB3, driving back the Bishop with gain of time.

### *3.* ...                                P × P

After this move, White gains a little ground in the centre and,
indeed, she might well have played *3.* N–QB3, and arrived at the
same position. This exchange of pawns is an attempt at simplifi-
cation, since it leaves White with little choice as to how to continue if she wishes to regain her pawn. It is doubtful whether it is
better than the logical continuation, *3.* ..., P–QB4; and there
is this to be said against it: it relieves White of the problem as to
how to develop her QB which was shut in by White's third move.

### *4.* N × P                                N–Q2

Why does she play this move rather than the natural *4.* ...,
N–KB3? The answer is that *4.* ..., N–KB3 is too natural a

continuation. For White could then play 5. N × N ch, Q × N; 6. N–B3, threatening to disturb the Queen by 7. B–N5, and thus to win time and space.

> 5. N–KB3

White proceeds with her development and, as I have pointed out in Chapter 6, it is nearly always advisable to develop Knights before developing the Bishops, since the Knight is a slow-stepping, but none the less powerful, piece.

> 5. ...          KN–B3
> 6. N × N ch      N × N

The point of Black's fourth move now becomes apparent. Had she not played a preliminary 4. ..., N–Q2, Black would now be forced to play either 6. ..., P × N, breaking up her King-side pawns, or else 6. ..., Q × N, when White could have gained time by attacking the Queen with 7. B–N5.

> 7. B–Q3

Here the Bishop is ideally placed to attack the enemy King, once it is castled on the King-side.

> 7. ...          B–K2
> 8. Q–K2

Another strong attacking move; on K2 the Queen is ready to join in the attack, as it can use its open line on the K file to attack the Black King, as will soon become apparent.

But there is also another point to this Queen manoeuvre. White wants to castle Queen-side and so have an even stronger attack on the other wing. The point here is that, once the White King has itself left the King-side, the pawns on the King-side can advance and join in the attack without fear of rendering the White King itself open and vulnerable to attack.

> 8. ...          O–O
> 9. B–KN5        R–N1

Black would like to develop her QB by 9. ..., P–QN3 and 10. ..., B–N2; but she sees that if 9. ..., P–QN3 is played at once, White can win by *10.* B × N, B × B; *11.* Q–K4, with a double attack – on KR7 and on QR8.

|  |  |  |
|---|---|---|
| *10.* O–O–O | | P–QN3 |
| *11.* P–KR4 | | |

A move she would have been reluctant to play, had her King been castled on the King-side. But, as will soon be seen, this advanced KRP will now form the firm basis for White's attack.

|  |  |  |
|---|---|---|
| *11.* ... | | B–N2 |
| *12.* K–N1 | | |

A useful precaution to take before launching out on the final attack. The King is moved still further from the centre in order to avoid it falling victim to an enemy counter-attack.

|  |  |  |
|---|---|---|
| *12.* ... | | R–B1 |

A serious waste of time from which Black never recovers. Much better was *12.* ..., P–KR3, not so much with the objective of driving the enemy Bishop away but with the idea of giving the Black King breathing space and possible (eventual) refuge from the enemy attack on KR2.

A possible alternative is *12.* ..., B × N; *13.* Q × B, Q–Q4; and not *13.* ..., Q × P; *14.* B × P ch, winning Black's Queen.

However, after *14.* Q–K2, Black must not play *14.* ..., Q × NP; since then *15.* KR–N1, Q–Q4; *16.* P–QB4, Q–R4; *17.* P–Q5, would leave Black helpless against the many threats.

But this line would always be bad for Black, since White's two Bishops are powerful in the attack, and in any case White would always have the strong manoeuvre P–QB4 and P–Q5 at her disposal.

|  |  |  |
|---|---|---|
| *13.* B × N | | |

Eliminating the Knight which is usually the best piece to defend the King; but White is also preparing a sacrificial combination to destroy Black's King's position.

| 13. ... | B × B |
|---------|-------|
| 14. B × P ch | |

The point of this sacrifice is that it allows White's Queen and Knight to join in on the attack on the enemy King.

| 14. ... | K–R1 |
|---------|------|

This rejection of the sacrifice does not and cannot save Black from losing.

But Black also loses after *14.* ..., K × B; *15.* N–N5 ch and if

(*a*) *15.* ..., B × N; *16.* P × B dis ch, K–N3 (or *16.* ..., K–N1; *17.* Q–R5, P–KB3; *18.* P–N6, and White mates next move by Q–R8); *17.* Q–R5 ch, K–B4; *18.* KR–K1, B–K5; *19.* P–B3, Q × NP (other moves are equally hopeless for Black; note how wise the precaution of *12.* K–N1 was, since otherwise Black could have saved herself by Q × P ch here); *20.* P × B ch, K–B5; *21.* Q–B3 mate.

Or (*b*) *15.* ..., K–N1; *16.* Q–R5, B–K5; *17.* N × B, R–K1; *18.* N–N5, B × N; *19.* P × B, K–B1; *20.* Q–R8 ch, K–K2; *21.* Q × P, R–B1; *22.* P–Q5, and Black's position is hopeless.

Or (*c*) *15.* ..., K–R3; *16.* Q–K3, K–R4 (White was threatening N × BP double check); *17.* P–N4 ch, K × P; *18.* Q–K2 ch, K–B4; *19.* Q–Q3 ch, K–N5 (if *19.* ..., K–B5; *20.* N–R3 ch, K–N5; *21.* QR–N1 ch, and mates in a few moves); *20.* QR–N1 ch, K–B5 (or *20.* ..., K–R4; *21.* Q–R7 mate); *21.* N–R3 mate.

Or (*d*) *15.* ..., K–N3; *16.* Q–Q3 ch, K–R4; *17.* P–N4 ch, K × P; *18.* QR–N1 ch, K–B5; *19.* N–R3 mate.

| *15.* B–Q3 | B × N |
|---|---|

To prevent White from playing N–N5 with variations similar to those given in the long note after Black's fourteenth move.

If, instead, *15.* ..., B × P; *16.* N × B, Q × N; *17.* Q–R5 ch, K–N1; *18.* Q–R7 mate.

| *16.* Q × B | Q–Q4 |
|---|---|

Or *16.* ..., P–N3; *17.* P–R5, P–KN4; *18.* Q–K4, and White mates on R7.

| *17.* B–K4 | Q–QR4 |
|---|---|
| *18.* P–Q5 | resigns. |

With the Black Queen thus cut off from the King-side, Black's position is hopeless: for example, *18.* ..., KR–Q1; *19.* R–R3, P × P; *20.* B–B5, R–QN1; *21.* Q–R5 ch, K–N1; *22.* R–K3, P–N3; *23.* B × P, P × B; *24.* Q × NP ch, B–N2; *25.* R–K7, and Black is going to be mated.

### GAME 2

Played in Round Five of the 'Man and His World' Chess Challenge Cup international grandmaster tournament at Montreal, 1979.

WHITE: M. TAL      BLACK: B. LARSEN
(Sicilian Defence)

| *1.* P–K4 | P–QB4 |
|---|---|

The Sicilian Defence, certainly the most popular defence to the King's Pawn opening, not only now but also in the past. See Chapter 7, page 126.

| *2.* N–KB3 | N–QB3 |
|---|---|

The main alternative is *2.* ..., P–Q3. See Chapter 7, page 126. The move actually chosen, being an active developing one, is very much to Bent Larsen's taste, the Danish grandmaster being, above everything, a dynamic, active player.

### 3. P–Q4

Likewise a normal opening procedure. White strikes in the centre before Black can prevent him from so doing by such moves as P–KN3 and B–N2.

### 3. ...                                   P × P

Black must make this exchange, since otherwise White would gain space and time by P–Q5.

### 4. N × P                              N–B3

Black must not exchange off Knights here since, after 4. ..., N × N; 5. Q × N, White's Queen is beautifully placed in the centre and Black can only disturb it by playing 5. ..., P–Q3 and 6. ..., P–K4; and this would leave Black with a nasty backward pawn on Q3, which in turn would mean that White would have good chances of establishing a Knight on his Q5.

### 5. N–QB3

A mistake would be 5. N × N, NP × N; 6. P–K5, on account of 6. ..., Q–R4 ch, when Black will pick up the enemy KP with check. But now that White has developed his Knight to QB3, Black no longer can play Q–R4 ch, and White is really threatening N × N followed by P–K5, disturbing the enemy KN. So Black now guards this square.

### 5. ...                                   P–Q3
### 6. B–KN5

Threatening to break up Black's pawn formation on the King-side by B × N. Hence Black's next move, which means that if White plays B × N, Black can simply retake with the Queen.

### 6. ...                                   P–K3
### 7. Q–Q2

Bringing the Queen and Bishop into co-operation – always a

good idea, since these two pieces work wonderfully well together – and preparing to castle Queen-side.

7. ...                                    B–K2

A good developing move that seems to prepare to castle his King on the King-side.

8. O–O–O                                  P–QR3

This pawn move is a useful precaution in defence, since it prevents the enemy Knight from going to N5 and also protects his Queen from attack when it goes to B2. It is also a useful attacking weapon since it prepares an eventual P–QN4.

9. P–B4                                    Q–B2

This was clearly Black's intention with his previous move; the idea is that if now 10. B × N, P × B; and not 10. ..., B × B; 11. N × N, Q × N; 12. Q × P, but a preferable line to the Queen move would have been 9. ..., B–Q2; followed by P–QN4.

10. B–K2                                   N × N

This plan of campaign is wrong, since it allows White to control the centre and gain command of K5. Better was 10. ..., O–O or, returning to the idea given in the previous note, 10. ..., B–Q2.

A game played in the U.S.S.R. in 1963 between Gruzman and Belinkov continued here 10. ..., O–O; 11. B–B3, R–Q1; 12. P–KN4, R–N1; 13. Q–N2, B–Q2; 14. B–R4, N × N; 15. R × N, P–QN4; 16. P–N5, N–K1; 17. P–B5, P–N5; with each side having chances against the enemy King.

11. Q × N                                  P–N4

After this the storm bursts, and White is able to launch an immediate attack in the centre. But Black has not an easy problem to solve here. If, for example, 11. ..., O–O; 12. B × N, and Black has to play 12. ..., P × B if he wishes to avoid the loss of a pawn. Or if 11. ..., Q–B3; 12. B–B3, threatening P–K5 with redoubled effect. Best seems *11* ..., B–Q2; hoping for time to play B–B3.

> 12. P–K5

Former world champion Tal is noted for his dynamic play, and this game is typical of his keenness to attack. With this pawn thrust he opens up the lines not only vertically but also diagonally, in particular along the long diagonal from KR1 to QR8.

> 12. ...          P × P
> 13. P × P          N–Q4
> 14. B × B

Forced, and forcing; in any case he cannot play *14.* N × N, B × B ch.

> 14. ...          N × N

The only move; if *14.* ..., N × B; *15.* N × P, P × N; *16.* B × P ch, and Black must return the piece with interest in the shape of two pawns. Quicker, from the point of view of despatch of one's opponent, is *14.* ..., N × B; *15.* N × P, P × N; *16.* B × P ch, K–B1; *17.* Q–Q8 ch, followed by mate.

> 15. B–B3

183

A bewildering position; there are three main possibilities:
(*a*) *15.* ..., K × B; *16.* P × N, B–N2; *17.* Q–Q6 ch, Q × Q; *18.* P × Q ch, and Black loses a piece.

(*b*) *15.* ..., N–K7 ch; *16.* B × N, Q × B; *17.* B–B3, B–N2;
*18.* B × B, Q × B; *19.* Q–Q6, R–QB1; *20.* R–Q2, Q–B3; *21.*
KR–Q1, Q × Q; *22.* R × Q, R–R1; *23.* R–N6, P–KR4; *24.*
R(Q1)–Q6, P–R5; *25.* R × RP, R × R; *26.* R × R, R–R4; thus
far Larsen in the tournament bulletin; the Yugoslav grandmaster,
Gligoric, adds the following line: *27.* R–R5, R × P; *28.* P–R4,
R–K7; *29.* P × P, R × P; *30.* P–N6, K–Q2; *31.* R–QB5, a
variation that wins easily for White.

(*c*) The move Black actually plays which loses quickly.

|       |         |            |
|-------|---------|------------|
| *15.* | ...     | N × R      |
| *16.* | B–Q6    | Q–B5       |

Or *16.* ..., Q–R2; *17.* B–B5.

|       |         |            |
|-------|---------|------------|
| *17.* | Q–N6    |            |

The Black King is held in a vice-like grip with the dominating
Bishop on Q6 preventing any release for the King.

|       |           |          |
|-------|-----------|----------|
| *17.* | ...       | N–B7     |
| *18.* | B–B6 ch   | B–Q2     |
| *19.* | B × B ch  | K × B    |
| *20.* | Q–N7 ch   | K–Q1     |
| *21.* | Q × R ch  | Q–B1     |
| *22.* | Q–R7      | resigns. |

Since White is threatening both Q–K7 mate and Q × N. He
cannot fend off both threats.

### GAME 3

Played in an international tournament at Munich, 1979.

WHITE: B. SPASSKY      BLACK: G. SIGURJONSSON
(Queen's Pawn,
Queen's Indian Defence)

|          |           |
|----------|-----------|
| *1.* P–Q4 | N–KB3    |

The usual move nowadays; it is a non-committal move and yet
at the same time it controls White's K4 and therefore fulfils an
important central function.

| 2. P–QB4 | P–K3 |
|---|---|

Allowing the KB a diagonal on which to develop and giving him some hold on the centre. Eventually he contemplates confronting White in the centre by P–Q4.

### 3. N–KB3

White replies to a non-committal Knight move with another such move. But this Knight too has central tendencies and is aimed at K5, as will be seen later on.

Had he played here 3. N–QB3, we could have had a Nimzo-Indian Defence by 3. ..., B–N5; see Chapter 6, page 145.

| 3. ... | P–QN3 |
|---|---|

Black decides to go in for a Queen's Indian Defence which, by fianchettoing the QB, helps Black to control the vital central square on White's K4. It is a sound defence, as witness its adoption by such great players as Alekhine and Capablanca. But it needs the most accurate handling if the second player wishes to avoid early disaster.

### 4. P–K3

White could have adopted a counter-fianchetto by P–KN3 and B–N2; but experience has shown that Black can equalize the game without much trouble against this method of play, and the humble pawn move allows White to build up a system with great potential attacking possibilities.

| 4. ... | B–N2 |
|---|---|
| 5. B–Q3 | B–K2 |
| 6. O–O | O–O |

Both sides tuck their King away on the flank before considering how to gain the upper hand in the centre.

### 7. P–QN3

Here the Bishop will be able to join in on the battle for White's K5 and, as will eventually become clear, this pressure along the black squares is all-important.

7. ...                                    P–Q4

A doubtful move, since it abandons without a fight the vital K5 (White's) square.

Preferable was 7. ..., P–B4; followed by a further strengthening of the black squares by P–Q3.

8. B–N2                              QN–Q2
9. N–B3                              P–B4

Writing in the *British Chess Magazine* a few months later, the international master, Bill Hartston, criticizes this move, but the continuation he advises (N–K5, with an eventual P–KB4) suffers from the drawback that White can always play N–Q2, followed by P–B3.

10. Q–K2

A strong centralizing move that enables White to switch the Queen over to the flank on either side, according to where the main attack is to be directed.

10. ...                              BP × P

Spassky himself, playing with the Black pieces against the great Estonian master, Paul Keres, at Göteborg, 1955, played here 10. ..., QP × P; *11*. NP × P, Q–B2; but had to endure a terrific attack after *12*. QR–Q1, QR–Q1; *13*. P–Q5, P × P; *14*. P × P, N × P; *15*. N × N, B × N; *16*. B × P ch, K × B; *17*. R × B, N–B3; *18*. R–N5.

*11*. KP × P

Notice that with the exchange of pawns White's control of K5 becomes enhanced, and it is this control that will prove to be a decisive factor in the attack against the enemy King.

*11*. ...                              R–K1

A good strategic idea; he plans to bring his KB back to B1 and then develop it by a sort of delayed fianchetto on KN2.

|        |        |
| ------ | ------ |
| *12.* QR–Q1 | B–KB1 |
| *13.* N–K5 | P–KN3 |
| *14.* P–B4 | R–B1 |

184

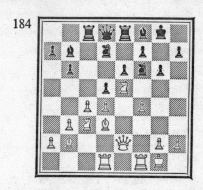

A critical point in the game has been reached. If Black's defensive plan is correct then *14.* . . ., B–N2 should be playable here. But he then runs into trouble after *15.* N–N5, N–B1; *16.* B–R3, when N–K5 fails against *17.* B × N, P × B; *18.* N–Q6.

> *15.* R–B2

If *15.* Q–K3 at once, then *15.* . . ., N–B4; when *16.* P × N, loses the Queen after *16.* . . ., B × P.

|        |        |
| ------ | ------ |
| *15.* . . . | N–N1 |
| *16.* Q–K3 | N–B3 |
| *17.* B–K2 |  |

One of the charms of this game is the way White unites tactical skill with a really consummate positional mastery. Now the plan is to play B–KB3 and, by a series of exchanges, to eliminate Black's best minor piece, the B on QN2, and then to switch the attack over to the King-side.

|        |        |
| ------ | ------ |
| *17.* . . . | B–N5 |

Not a good move, but Black has run short of good moves in a position where his strategy has been disproved.

211

| | |
|---|---|
| *18.* B–B3 | N–QR4 |
| *19.* P × P | N × QP |

And not *19.* ..., B × N; when *20.* P × P, wins at least a pawn, since he cannot play *20.* ..., B × P; on account of *21.* P × P ch, and Black's position collapses like the proverbial house of cards.

| | |
|---|---|
| *20.* N × N | B × N |

Or *20.* ..., P × N; *21.* P–B5, P–KN4; *22.* P–B6, and White wins.

| | |
|---|---|
| *21.* B × B | Q × B |

Again if *21.* ..., P × B; *22.* P–B5 is crushing.

*22.* N–N4

A very strong move that takes full advantage of Black's weaknesses on the King-side. The immediate threat is N–B6 ch.

| | |
|---|---|
| *22.* ... | B–K2 |
| *23.* B–R3! | |

Beautiful play; if now *23.* ..., B × B; *24.* N–B6 ch.

| | |
|---|---|
| *23.* ... | Q–R4 |
| *24.* P–R3 | B–R5 |
| *25.* R–K2 | |

Suddenly Black finds himself faced with the terrible threat of a thrust in the centre by P–Q5.

| | |
|---|---|
| *25.* ... | P–B4 |
| *26.* N–K5 | R–B6 |

Desperately ingenious; but the logic of the position is against him.

| | |
|---|---|
| *27.* Q × R | Q × R |
| *28.* R–QB1 | R–Q1 |

White was threatening P–QN4, N–N2; Q–B6.

| 29. Q–B7 | Q–B7 ch |
| 30. K–R1 | Q × BP |
| 31. Q–B7 ch | K–R1 |
| 32. N–B3 | resigns. |

White's threat of R–B7 cannot be averted; a magnificent game and an anthology piece that deserves the utmost study.

### EXERCISES

185

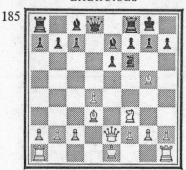

Black to play

1. What happens if Black plays 9. ..., P–QN3?

186

White to play

2. What should White play here?

187

White to play

3. Why not 5. N × N, NP × N; 6. P–K5 here?

188

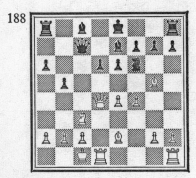

4. How should White continue the attack here?

189

Black to play

5.  What happens after *14.* ..., B–N2 here?

190

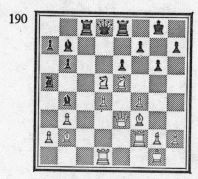

Black to play

6.  Why not *20.* ..., P × N?

## ANSWERS TO THE EXERCISES

1. (see Diagram 185) White wins after *9.* ..., P–QN3; by *10.* B × N, B × B; *11.* Q–K4, with a double attack on KR7 and QR8.

2. (see Diagram 186) White should play *12.* K–N1. When White has castled Queen-side it is always useful to play this move to avoid any sudden attacks either on the QB file or on the diagonal QB1–KR6.

3. (see Diagram 187) Because of *6.* ..., Q–R4 ch; picking up the pawn.

4. (see Diagram 188) By *12.* P–K5.

5. (see Diagram 189) White replies *15.* N–N5, N–B1; *16.* B–R3, nd if *16.* ..., N–K5; *17.* B × N) (K4), P × B; *18.* N–Q6.

6. (see Diagram 190) Because of *21.* P–B5, P–KN4; *22.* P–B6.

# CHAPTER 12

# HOW TO IMPROVE

So far so good; indeed, if you have gained some inkling as to how the mind of a great player works from studying the games in Chapter 11, you must have developed some comprehension of the game and, in chess, understanding is more than half the battle.

I have taught, or tried to teach, many people how to play chess and how to improve their game; in the final instance, it has always been a matter of understanding. So really, when I write 'how to improve your chess', I mean, how to better your understanding of the game. Once this is achieved, everything else – knowledge, skill and effectiveness as a player – will follow with some ease. Chess is an easy game to learn, a difficult one to understand, and an easy game to play well, once this understanding is there.

How, then, to improve? You will not, I think, have much chance of improving by solitary study. True, this is possible if you are a Paul Morphy, a Capablanca or a Bobby Fischer, and even if I concede you are one or all of these three, I would point out that these three great players had to play against other players before they became the wonderful players they are.

You should therefore seek out another player of about the same degree of chess strength as yourself (preferably one a little, but not too much, better than yourself) and practise the game with him. A year-long match, to determine who is the better and by how much, is a fine idea. Even more helpful is to get together with your partner to play out all sorts of chess endings, not only those given in this book but a wide variety of other endings. You will be surprised how much this will improve your play. You should also get hold of the games of great players and try and work out for yourself what is the reason for their moves. Later on in this chapter I give you a list of books that should be helpful in this respect.

217

The next step would be to join a chess club and play in tournaments and matches. If you are a junior and still at school, university or some scholastic establishment, then you should find there is a ready-made club there at your disposal. This should also apply if you are working, in a business, factory or any avocation ranging from farming to bus-conducting, and equally there should be no difficulty in finding a chess club if you are a member of a profession, a teacher, a lawyer or a doctor. If you are a politician you will no doubt already know that chess is the only game permitted in the House of Commons.

If all else fails and you find you are working or studying in a place where there is no chess club, then you will be able to have recourse to one of two operations. You can demonstrate your powers of organization by setting up a chess club, thereby killing a number of birds with one stone. Or you can buy a copy of the British Chess Federation Yearbook in which you will find listed most of the chess clubs in the U.K., along with addresses, times of play, etc. The address to write to for a Yearbook is as follows: Mr Paul Buswell, General Secretary, British Chess Federation, 4 The Close, Norwich NR1 4DH (telephone number 0603 612678).

You will then discover that the British Chess Federation holds a yearly Congress, at which tournaments of all strengths are played. In addition, there are many congresses played throughout the year all over the country, and you would indeed be unlucky if one such congress were not to take place somewhere near you, at least in the same county in which you are resident.

Practice in such events is essential if you wish to continue to make progress at the game. Nor need you be discouraged if, in your first effort, you do badly. Many a future champion came bottom in his first open tournament.

It is one of the many delights of chess that it is a literate game for literate people, and this means that a good book on chess is almost inevitably a pleasure to read. Here, therefore, follows a list of further reading which I think you will find both enjoyable and profitable.

A suitable general book is H. Golombek, *The Game of Chess*, a Penguin handbook which is aimed not only at beginners but is also suitable for those who already know something about the game.

For the games of great masters, I would recommend Alekhine's *My Best Games of Chess, 1908–23* which provides as rich feeding as the chess mind can hope for; H. Golombek's *Capablanca's Best Games of Chess* for classically serene play; Fischer's *My 60 Memorable Games*, which are truly memorable, despite the occasionally gauche language; and Paul Keres' *Grandmaster of Chess*, in which the annotations are as marvellous as the games.

For the openings: R. C. Griffiths and H. Golombek, *Pocket Guide to the Openings* and A. P. Sokolsky, *The Modern Openings in Theory and Practice*.

For the middle game: P. Keres and A. Kotov, *The Art of the Middle Game* (particularly remarkable for the way Keres reveals the workings of the mind of a grandmaster). Also A. Nimzovitch, *My System*, which is a wonderful collection of what one might call tactical ideas.

For the end game: D. A. Hooper, *A Pocket Guide to the End-Games* and, later on, R. Fine, *Basic Chess Endings*.

For interest and enjoyment, with some instruction artfully intertwined, Réti's *Modern Ideas in Chess*; and for the history of chess (which happens to be a subject of entrancing interest) H. Golombek, *A History of Chess*. There is also *The Penguin Encyclopedia of Chess*, which is published in the Penguin handbook series.

# INDEX